SpringerBriefs in Law

More information about this series at http://www.springer.com/series/10164

Paulo Ferreira da Cunha

Political Ethics and European Constitution

Springer

Paulo Ferreira da Cunha
Faculty of Law
University of Porto
Porto
Portugal

and

School of Law
University Anhembi Morumbi
(Laureate International Universities)
São Paulo
Brazil

ISSN 2192-855X ISSN 2192-8568 (electronic)
SpringerBriefs in Law
ISBN 978-3-662-45599-9 ISBN 978-3-662-45600-2 (eBook)
DOI 10.1007/978-3-662-45600-2

Library of Congress Control Number: 2014958895

Springer Heidelberg New York Dordrecht London

Printed on acid-free paper

Springer-Verlag GmbH Berlin Heidelberg is part of Springer Science+Business Media
(www.springer.com)

To the Founding Fathers of Europe
D.D.D.

Sources

This book takes inspiration from some previous work, mainly my book Para uma Ética Constitucional, Lisbon, Coisas de Ler, 2010 and some miscellaneous articles.

Preface

A most stimulating intellectual exercise, from the perspective of cultural history and philosophy, is to examine the main *aporia* of Law, that is, of legal thinking: Law and legal thinking seek to base themselves on the same human territory of legality and historicity from which, at this very moment, dare to reformulate or refound the bases of another *illud tempus*, an ought (*Sollen*) for which we do not have the ontological answer, though we may already formulate the ethical questions.

Law and thinking about law are occurring in the present or the near future, and without such an aspiration these texts would remain a dead letter, thinking without thought. Between the world that is and the expected one, about which there are only outlines, lies a ravine of deep meanings. Approaching from the proper direction, but in order to build the bridges, it is recognized that the path is narrow and hard to run which, more properly, could be called here by philosophical operation.

In this journey the traveler or investigator focuses on the primary question residing at the intersection of the fields of political philosophy and axiology. One of the warning signs, written by Cartesius and then implanted in the *Aufklärung*, warns that the land is undermined by the teleological perfection which the old theology and metaphysics were unable to explain. To brave it, we must demine the field, remove traps and secularize the envisioned promised land, in the careful limits of the ethical assumption of Being and its weight, that is, in an objectifying dimension of a political ethos.

It is no wonder that this book, authored by Prof. Paulo Ferreira da Cunha, reads like a brief and concise treatise on the contemporary *respublicana virtù* and in its broadest sense as an instruction manual for the good management of public affairs. But its brevity is misleading: it is first and foremost an important contribution because of its epistemological implications and its bold proposals—that place the *Libertas*, the essential breath in the house of being at the apex of the study. Breathing, in whose light the constituents of the revolutionary triad horizons of 1789 are readable, and from which emerge the dreams of equality and fraternity that the quarrels of humanism, antihumanism and posthumanism failed to destroy.

The author searches for the foundation of freedom in that sensitive intelligence (X. Zubiri) full of *pathos*, which allows us to understand how to overcome the double Cartesian and Pascalian limitation. At the root of this *pathos* kindness, the gift, the material disinterest pervades Reason, emphasizing Spinozistic intellectual love, and consolidating its foundation which is at last able to federate or confederate differences, disconnections, arrhythmias, ignorance, hatred and to overcome them. In the court of the temple of their own history, only one sensible reason can illuminate the steps of men on the path of time.

Finally, what should be said at the beginning: reader, please note that this text is not a *anteloquium*, a preface to the book. For the book itself, this book in particular, is a Morning text (and *Morganrötte*) that constitutes a *praefactio* to a world that is under construction and to be discovered, but whose morning aroma sometimes (and so rare are the sites of world where a fresh dawn becomes breathable) instills the beautiful future memory of an ontological revelation which is "to-do" (*Bildung*).

It is this question of Being that the indefatigable researcher, animated by an inexhaustible *libido sciendi*, articulates clearly, precisely—and with great mastery in this *Libretto*. As for the sound of the symphony, the supreme harmonious aspiration, nothing implies it: only by moving forward can each one of us hear the unexpected Melody.

Paulo Archer de Carvalho
Investigator, Interdisciplinary
Studies Center of the Twentieth Century
University of Coimbra, FCT—Post Doctoral
Studies in Contemporary History of Culture

Contents

About the Author

Paulo Ferreira da Cunha (1959) is a Member of the ad hoc comittee for an International Constitutional Court. He is a full Professor (with tenure) at the Law Faculty of the University of Porto, he holds two Ph.Ds in Law: from the University of Paris II and the University of Coimbra. He is also a postdoc at the Faculty of Law of the University of São Paulo, Brazil, an Associate Professor at Laurentian University, Canada, Honorary Professor at Mackenzie University, Professor at the Académie Internationale de Droit Constitutionnel and Visiting Professor at São Paulo University and of the Kiev Faculty of Law at the Ukrainian National Academy of Sciences. He is a member of The Juridical Letters Academy of São Paulo, among other scientific societies. He has published more than 100 books and 500 articles in 12 languages, and he is a director of various international journals, such as the *International Studies on Law and Education*. In 2007 he won the Jabuti Prize for the best book on Law, with his book *Direito Constitucional Geral* (*General Constitutional Law*). He won a scholarship from FUNADESP to study Law Fundamentals and International Constitutional Contract, and he is Professor of University Anhembi-Morumbi (Laureate International Universities), and Full Professor of FADISP—Faculdade Autônoma de Direito, São Paulo, Brazil.

Chapter 1
Introduction

The European crisis, which began as a financial, then economic and social crisis, is now a political and constitutional one as well. In some countries constitutions are already dead letter at the economic and social levels, and within the superstructure of the European Union, cohesion is thus endangered. The crisis has placed all other issues out of the spotlight. The very question of the European Constitution is invoked only timidly before the imperative of immediate action, and the average European citizen is confronted with bad news everyday since social unrest in Greece or Spain is equally disconcerting for the Germans, the English, or the French—we are all in the same boat: prosperity or ruin is our common fate. It is only a matter of time. There hasn't been much debate on the European constitutional arrangement in these times when we are practically at war and our energies are spent trying to do triage on immediate emergencies.

In this book, we propose to study the deeper roots of European political and ethical problems and constitutional questions. The casino economy and the levity of those to whom we deliver our money (some banks and governments) and who play irresponsibly and may be even criminally with our lives, is nothing but a manifestation of the moral crisis we have been living under for a long time.

This is a crisis that has forgotten the values and virtues of the Republic, an ideal that, however, has been revived in certain intellectual sectors of our societies. There is, of course, a need for sound financial and economic measures—and before these, political measures and decisions—that can save us all from the abyss that some claim is certain. We are confident that there is a way to avoid that abyss by reversing the policy of austerity, and many authorities, starting with Nobel Laureates, have insisted that Europe should reverse this course, though, unfortunately, governments and the supranational institutions generally don't listen to these opinions. But at the heart of everything is the need for societies to turn to political values and virtues. Not, of course, the values and virtues that old-fashioned or hypocritical virtues which, as Paul Valery suggests, would make our contemporaries smile. But it is a matter of more perennial ethics, i.e., of republican ethics. With all the adaptations that the times dictate. Not only sociologically, but also ethically.

P. Ferreira da Cunha, *Political Ethics and European Constitution*,
SpringerBriefs in Law, DOI 10.1007/978-3-662-45600-2_1

In fact, Republican Ethics is no longer only a mystic of dedication and service to the *Res Publica*, a set of simple republican virtues with which to impregnate the State itself through the Constitution. Today's constitutions emphasize republican values above all, implicitly (the Spanish, in Art. 1, 1, or the Croatian, in Art. 2, 3, explicitly), and begin to stress the need for republican virtues as well.

The Republic is an ethical democracy, not only a technical[1] democracy. It is not only about the democratic veneer, it is about democratic substance. It is not only a ritual of voting and electing representatives, etc. All of that has to make sense, and all of that needs to be done in the community interest and aspire to the common good.[2] Just as governance has to be strictly devoted to the public interest, with all that implies.[3]

Europe and its Constitution—its real Constitution, present in *the praxis* of European law and politics—may only survive if it puts aside its logic of monetary values and greedy virtues, and embraces the way of true republican ethics. A utopia? Let us quote the neoliberals, *pro domo nostra*: "**T**here **I**s **N**o **A**lternative." TINA is back, this time it is on the other side: the side of the Republic and Ethics.

References

Anderheiden, M. (2003). Verfassungsrechtliche Potentiale des Republikprinzips. *Berliner Debatte Initial*, 14.

Bigotte Chorão, M. (1986). *Introdução a Temas Fundamentais de Direito*. Coimbra: Almedina.

Ehrhardt Soares, R. (1959). *Interesse Público, Legalidade e Mérito*. Coimbra: Atlântida.

Ferreira da Cunha, P. (2005). *Política Mínima* (2nd ed.). Coimbra: Almedina.

Groeschner, R. (2004). § 23. In J. Isensee & P. Kirchhof (Eds.), *Handbuch des Staatsrechts der Bundesrepublik Deutschland II, Verfassungsstaat* (3rd ed.). Heidelberg: C.F. Mueller.

Koslowski, P. (Ed.). (1999). *Das Gemeinwohl zwischen Universalismus und Particularismus zur Theorie des Gemeinwohls und der Gemeinwohlwirkung von Ehescheidung, politischer Sezession und Kirchentrennung*. Stuttgart: Frommann-Holzboog.

Montoro Ballesteros, A. (1979). *Razones y limites de la legitimación democrática del Derecho*. Murcia: Universidad de Murcia.

Rousseau, D. (2007). *La V. e République se meurt, vive la démocratie*. Paris: Odile Jacob.

Schachtscheiner, K.-A. (1994). *Res publica res populi. Grundlegung einer Allgemeinen Republiklehre. Ein Beitrag zur Freiheits-Rechts-und Staatslehre*. Berlin: Duncker und Humblot.

Tzitzis, S. (2012/2013). Crise économique, souveraineté populaire et droits sociaux. In: *Annuaire Internional des Drois de l'homme* (vol. 7, pp. 505 *et sq.*).

---

[1] Montoro Ballesteros (1979), and Bigotte Chorão (1986). To oppose democracy to the republic does not seem a good conceptual procedure. If a republic is really very bad in what concerns at least fundamental rights, it wouldn't be a real republic. If "republic" cannot be "replaced" for a "democracy" everything is wrong, although the concepts are not alike … at least, in today's conceptualization. Cf., in a controversial perspective, Rousseau (2007); New perspectives, Tzitzis (2012/2013).

[2] See Schachtscheiner (1994), Anderheiden (2003), pp. 45 et sq., Groeschner (2004), § 23, Rn. 34 et sq. The connotations of the "common good" vary, as well as its concept. See, in general, Ferreira da Cunha (2005), pp. 92 et sq., Koslowski (1999).

[3] A classic treatise on the public interest question in a legal context is the masterwork of Ehrhardt Soares (1959). It is always important, when we are theorizing politically, not to forget that many of the great concepts of politics have a legal basis, which can be a source of inspiration, in one way or another.

Chapter 2
Political Virtues

ce qui ne signifie pas que, dans une certaine république, on soit vertueux; mais qu'on devroit l'être. Cela ne prouve pas non plus que, dans une certaine monarchie, on ait de l'honneur: et que, dans un État despotique particulier, on ait de la crainte; mais qu'il faudroit en avoir: sans quoi le gouvernement sera imparfait.

Montesquieu—De l'Esprit des Lois, III, 11.

2.1 No Republic Without Virtue

Nowadays, political ethics may be called, republican ethics in what concerns either virtues or values. The Republic is, furthermore, an ethical government, not just a political regime. Without virtue the Republic misrepresents itself and perishes:

> Lorsque cette vertu cesse, l'ambition entre dans les coeurs qui peuvent la recevoir, et l'avarice entre dans tous. Les désirs changent d'objets: ce qu'on aimait, on ne l'aime plus; on était libre avec les lois, on veut être libre contre ells. Chaque citoyen est comme un esclave échappé de la maison de son maître; ce qui était *maxime*, on l'appelle *rigueur*; ce qui était *règle,* on l'appelle *gêne;* ce qui y était *attention*, on l'appelle *crainte*. C'est la frugalité qui y est l'avarice, et non pas le désir d'avoir. Autrefois le bien des particuliers faisait le trésor public; mais pour lors le trésor public deviant le patrimoine des particuliers. La république est une dépouille; et sa force n'est plus que le pouvoir de quelques citoyens et la licence de tous.[1]

So, in this book we take political ethics and republican ethics as synonyms.

In ancient Greece, we originally had the σοφια (wisdom, which would recede in prudency), the σωφροσυνη (from which would temperance result), the strength, courage, or value (ανδρια), which would later be the Stronghold, then Justice (διακαιοσυνη), the most immutable of them all if we discount its own semantic evolution, which, in the Middle Ages led to identifying with the figure of Job or

[1] Montesquieu (1748), III, 3.

P. Ferreira da Cunha, *Political Ethics and European Constitution*,
SpringerBriefs in Law, DOI 10.1007/978-3-662-45600-2_2

with the figure of the merciful, or the defensive king of widows and orphans' (which has nothing to do with the Hellenic synonym, nor with the Roman meaning).[2]

2.2 Mythical Examples of Classical Virtues

Ancient Greece and Rome give us a considerable number of mythical and historical examples (also mythicized) of people who, one way or another, may be symbolic of classical virtues and of virtues in general.

Examples for Prudency: Fabius Maximus, Socrates and Numa Pompilius; for Justice, Camillus, Pittacus and Trajan; for Stronghold: Leonidas and Horatius Cocles; for Temperance: Scipio, Pericles, and Cincinnatus.

Marcus Furius Camillus (446–365 B.C) was one of those extraordinary Roman magistrates, called "dictators"—temporary and legally appointed magistrature, as was the custom then. Slandered, he preferred exile, but he would end up returning: faced with the *Vae victis* speech of Gaulish Breno, Rome's marauder, Camillus opposed him with another maxim that would remain famous: *Non auro, sed ferro, recuperando est patria.* And through the iron he would release the homeland from the invaders.

Pittacus de Mytilene (who lived in the seventh century B.C.) was considered as one of the seven Greek wise men. He challenged an institution with some similarity to Roman "dictatorship"—one of the tyrants, which, initially, as we know, hadn't any negative connotation, meaning only the lack of a normal title for exercising power. The wise Pittacus would depose the despotic governor of Mytilene, but instead of perpetuating himself in command, he retired after ruling for 10 years.

The Emperor Trajan (53–117) made himself distinguished in practically all domains, considered by some as the greatest Roman emperor. It is then natural that we consider him exemplary.

Leonidas died heroically in the Thermopile gorge (480 B.C.) accompanied by three hundred Spartans. History and legend tell of his bravery in his last fight against the Persians commanded by Xerxes.

The legend of Leonidas is similar to that of Publio Horatius Cocles' (sixth century B.C.), according to which he would have defended the bridge that led to Rome alone, defending it from the Etruscans, headed by Porsena.[3]

Publius Cornelius, Scipio African (236–183 B.C.) is a very complex figure, perhaps praised for his temperance since he knew how to appreciate his enemy Hannibal Barca and for the magnanimous way that, in general, he treated defeated Carthage. He died in exile, leaving this self-written epitaph: *Ingrata patria, non possidebis ossa mea.*

---

2 Villey (1982), pp. 107 et sq., p. 111.

3 Livy (Titus Livius Patavinus), *Ab Urbe Condita*, II, 9, 1 et sq.

Pericles (495–429 B.C.), considered the mythical father of Athenian democracy (which however was a gradual process, and was truthfully only partially democratic, as is well known[4]), distinguished himself in many fields. Maybe the reason for special praise of his temperance is explained by the fact that he never desired to abuse power, adopting a wise balance, of which his relations with Cimon, his political opponent, are an example.

To Pericles Thucydides attributed a mournful speech in honor of the Athens' heroes killed in combat, which is an exquisite oratory play, but above all interests us as portrait of the Athenian Republic.

Cincinnatus was another Roman "dictator", who took the nation from crisis to victory in only 16 days (471 B.C.), and after this deed returned to plowing his land as he did before.[5]

But there are many exemplary mythical actors beyond these.[6] In fact, we see the correspondence between virtues and illustrious men to be sometimes a bit forced. Not everyone, certainly, but at least some.

We can look at examples of "excessive virtue" as a kind of vice by exaggeration. For example: that of Horatio, who killed his own sister because she cried for her fiancé, an enemy of the Republic that he had just killed. Or that of Marcio Portius Cato (234–139 B.C.) who confessed that he only held his wife when it thundered—but the situation, however, left him of good humor (he said).

On the other hand, the deeds of Regulus and Mucius Scaevola are no doubt heroic, but cannot be interpreted as a vicious exaggeration, only as extremely virtuous.

Marcus Atilius Regulus honored the word given to the Carthaginian enemies returning to Cartago for the greatest tortures and for death, after he himself had proposed not to give in to the Punic proposals[7] in the Senate.

Gaius Mucius Scaevola is a mythical hero: surprised in his intent to kill the Etruscan leader Persena, he thrust his right hand into the flaming sacrificial brazier, showing not to have fear of death with which he had been threatened during the questioning. Astonished, the Etruscan released him.[8]

However, as Rousseau himself said, on preventing exaggeration:

> Les anciens peoples ne sont plus un modèle pour les moderns; ils leur sont trop étrangers à tous égards. Vous surtout, Genevois, gardez votre place, et n'allez point aux objets élevés, qu'on vous présente pour vous cacher l'abîme qu'on creuse au-devant de vous. Vous n'êtes ni Romains ni Spartiates, vous n'êtes pas même Athéniens. Laissez là ces grands noms, qui ne vous vont point. Vous êtes des marchands, des artisans, des bourgeois, toujours occupies

---

[4] Cf., about this classical subject, but always in renewal and inspiration for new questions, Jones (1986), Thorley (2004), Raaflaub et al. (2007), Palmer (1963), Finley (1976), Mossé (1993), da Rocha Pereira (1980), pp. 147 et sq. See still Vidal-Naquet (2002).

[5] Livy, *Ab Urbe Condita,* III, 26, 7 et sq.; da Rocha Pereira (1980), pp. 147 et sq.

[6] Matyszak and Berry (2008).

[7] Vallançon (1989), pp. 304–333.

[8] Livy, *Ab Urbe Condita*, II, 11, 1 et sq.

de leur interest privés, de leur travail, de leur traffic, de leur gain; des gens pour qui la liberté meme n'est qu'un moyen d'acquérir sans obstacle et de posséder en sûreté.[9]

Despite this, even Rousseau praised classical examples. Unfortunately, today classical culture has vanished from popular pursuit almost in its entirety, and the examples that we have given mean almost nothing to our youth. The republicans will have to search for ethics in the great sagas of contemporary literature: from *The Chronicles of Narnia,* to *The Lord of the Rings* and *Harry Potter* series.

But other sources, more explicitly political, may be proposed: like the excellent book of Fernando Pereira Marques, which echoes the thoughts of the philosopher and poet Antero de Quental, *Esboço de um Programa para os Trabalhos das Novas Gerações.*[10]

2.3 Postmodern Virtues

The "traditional" or classical virtues should certainly be joined by some others, not specifically political, but that seem essential to our times. We will call these—for our convenience but without excessive conviction—postmodern virtues.[11]

The Italian thinker and essayist Italo Calvino summed up some of these with sharpness and insight, in his "Charles Eliot Norton Poetry Lectures," which he sadly couldn't finish.[12]

From Calvino's English version, we shall also give them our interpretation, without implicating the author, who was merely an inspiration to our framework. Therefore, in our view, the following general virtues would be an essential support for republican virtues:

2.3.1 Lightness

The modern world is the *light* world,[13] for good and bad. It must have lightness, to have adaptability, ductility, and mental and experiential malleability. Not, obviously, to allow the so-called co-workers (giving the impression nobody is now a permanent employee) to shift from function to function, from land to land, deprived

---

[9] Rousseau (1764/1782–1789), electronic ed.:http://ftp.ac-toulouse.fr/pub/philosophie/rousseaulettre secritesdelamontagne.rtf-

[10] Pereira Marques (2002).

[11] See, even though in some way dated, Ferreira da Cunha (1991). More recently, *v.g.*, Bittar (2005), Chamon Junior (2007), Morrison (1997), Cotterrell (2003), pp. 237 et sq.; Douzinas and Gearey (2005), Ward (2004), pp. 155 et sq.

[12] Calvino (2002).

[13] Rojas (1994).

of their rights. But, it stresses the need to be permanently evolving, and adapting to change. It seems that the world where people held the same job and had the same specialty their whole lives has come to an end, as much as we would like it to be otherwise. It is a sad truth. We may try to work to rebuild the Welfare State in order to adapt to this new situation, but for now this has led to rising unemployment.

2.3.2 Agility (Quickness)

We know how in current times change has accelerated. It is necessary not to be totally detached nor a frenetic follower of trends and news, but, no doubt the resourcefulness that we require today has something to do with speed. Speed of understanding change, speed of responding to new challenges. We also believe that, first, we should cultivate an agility of spirit, with sharpness of thought. Even though—we shouldn't forget—with a "good use of slowness"[14]—as much as this is possible anyway.

2.3.3 Rigor (Precision)

We see, among our contemporaries, along with some growing "professionalism" (not always beneficial, because it tends toward exaggeration, to a lack of ductility and to a certain depersonalization), a lot of improvisation in ideas and acts. Precision, rigor, accuracy are essential. The amateur attitude among professionals needs to end. Of course, no offense to amateurs: there are some amateurs that do a lot of good. But amateurs are amateurs, and professionals are professionals.[15] A different matter is the love for his or her work that a real professional should have. But this love doesn't make him or her an amateur, on the contrary.

[14] Sansot (2000).

[15] For instance, we can't understand how social communication has so little rigor in what concerns the real qualification (not vague, alleged or consented) of some much-quoted professionals compared with those who have careers of the longest and most exigent of all: university professors. It is still an approximate form (and misleading to the public) that considers itself like a university professor in social communication (or, more subtly, with some euphemisms, depending on the language of course: nuances that the public in general obviously comprehends), using academic terminology like someone that teaches in a university. Even without an academic career, without special proofs provided, without titles beyond graduation (eventually these so-called "professors" may possess a Master's degree—but this isn't legally enough to qualify someone as a university "professor").

2.3.4 Exposure (Visibility)

In politics, as in many other fields, visibility has become increasingly indispensable. There is not (was there once in fact?) an omniscient entity that knows about people's values and awards merit. It may seem somewhat vulgar and even shocking, but some *marketing* is necessary: personal, institutional, etc. Those are the rules of the game. And as long as it is played with seriousness and some discretion (even with some elegance) there won't be an ethical mistake, or even a risk. This visibility is Protean: it goes from the need for some exposure and publicity, given the profusion of requites, from the very beginning until transparency, and institutional transparency, but trying to contradict today's voyeuristic society.[16]

2.3.5 Pluralism (Diversity)

The monism, confinement, crystallization, avarice and myopia that value only one area of knowledge, or one unique idea has its days numbered. For good and for bad, the current world is already very diverse, fragmentary[17] and plural[18] even in Law, which was normally a friend of the monist solutions, like legal positivism. There is always a need to have multiplicity, variety, pluralism, and interdisciplinarity in our knowledge.

2.3.6 Consistency

Even as a symmetric pole to variety and fragmentation, coherence and consistency are necessary—which needs to be the mortar of everything, because the future will be very demanding of articulation if a totalitarian concentration of power doesn't come and impose its boot on everything: and hopefully we still can avoid it, because we understand History and what happened before, after, and the reasons for such kinds of crisis.

2.3.7 "Un Coeur Intelligent"—"An Intelligent Heart"

Almost all these virtues refer to a very clear (affirmative, explicit) separation of the prejudice-paradigm from which the virtuous republican person is hard and fast, unable of adaptation, mentally heavy, slow, etc.—"conservative" even. To them we

[16] Débord (1940/2007).

[17] de Faria Costa (1993).

[18] Dembour (1990), pp. 43 et sq.

can add another from a poetic biblical passage, with a metaphor of the heart.[19] It is King Solomon that speaks:

> Give therefore thy servant an understanding heart to judge thy people, that I may discern between good and bad: for who is able to judge this thy great people?.[20]

About its relevance today Alain Finkielkraut comments:

> Le roi Salomon suppliait l'Éternel de lui accorder un coeur intelligent. Au sortir d'un siècle ravagé par les méfaits conjoints de la bureaucratie, c'est-à-dire d'une intelligence purement fonctionnelle, et de l'idéologie, c'est-à-dire d'une sentimentalité binaire et souverainement indifférente à la singularité des destins individuels, cette prière pour être doué de perspicacité affective a gardé toute sa valeur.[21]

Effectively, the twentieth century had in its non-"discrete" ideologies[22] (namely the fascists and the communists) terrible substitutive machines of critical thinking, and in the cadaveric hardness of the bureaucrats the source of one thousand incompetences and one thousand injustices. Without the affective intelligence (that refers to fraternity), we can't go far. On the other hand, with an intelligent heart, we go where reason and the heart alone don't allow.

2.4 The Virtue of *Auctoritas*

2.4.1 Consistency and Conviction

The first republican virtue demanded by today's challenges is true love of the Republic, and true love of its values: Freedom, Equality, Fraternity, and the pathways to them, like Solidarity and Justice. You cannot perform any public office well when this is done for one's own benefit, nor when the function is viewed with the cynicism of those who have no ideals, and none of these Republican ideals in particular. For example: at a certain moment, it was the lack of conviction, which dragged the lack of virtues, one of the main factors of corruption and fall of the Portuguese First Republic (1910–1926). It's not just to deploy the Republic, or dream about it. You have to live it, give it permanent cheer with acts of coherent belief. Let us recall the eloquent Edgar Quinet:

> (…) il ne suffit pas de dire devant le suffrage universel, au jour de l'élection : 'République ! République !' en pliant un genou. Nous demandons (…) des actes, des oeuvres conformes aux paroles.[23]

---

[19] Zambrano (1993), pp. 108 et sq.

[20] I R. III, 9: http://www.gospelhall.org/bible/bible.php?passage=1%20Kings+3&ver1=kjv.

[21] Finkielkraut (2009).

[22] Puy (1993).

[23] Quinet (2009), pp. 47.

2.4.2 Public Service and Dedication

Without a sense of mission (not self-investiture in the category, but the practice of real and devoted service) there is no *auctoritas* that would validate any *potestas*. But this myth of service cannot be confused with the rather different spirit of pseudo-mission of "providential men," which is a mythification. Republicans have always distrusted "providential men." This was the case of Ana de Castro Osório, in her mainly historical, but also civic (among other things) precious little book of elementary instruction:

> We do not need a saviour, we need many, who want to work and work to raise the Homeland.[24]

What it is about, and what is required for the Republic, is the spirit of service, statesmanship,[25] not just of one, but of many. José Adelino Maltez[26] judiciously quotes some passages from Alberto Morais António de Carvalho[27] on precisely the opposite of this republican spirit. We allow ourselves to glean:

> Employee with a small salary, living in luxury, if not inherited, stole. The positions of the state, in the hands of probity, give advantage, and honour: in the hands of corruption, give the benefit without honour. The probity of public employee cannot live, either in luxury, or in misery. Writers, ordinarily are like whores; they prostitute themselves to whoever pays them. If the honour of representing the nation by deputation was barren of jobs and distinctions, there would be fewer who have the ambition to represent. Despots never miss mandarins who are vile executors of their decrees. Any seaman is deemed qualified to steer the rudder of the ship of state, so she often suffers breakdowns. A wise government should create men for jobs not jobs for men. There are honours without honour, just as there is honour without honours.

2.4.3 Detachment from Public Places

It seems incredible to see politicians, throughout the world, clinging like limpets to power. Trying (and succeeding) to change the rules of the electoral game (usually through referendums, is always dangerous, a pasture of populism; some other times

[24] de Castro Osório (2008), pp. 92.

[25] See Ferreira da Cunha (2009), pp. 77 et sq.

[26] José Adelino Maltez, *blog Sobre o Tempo que Passa*: http://tempoquepassa.blogspot.com/.

[27] Morais de Carvalho (1850). Portuguese original: *O empregado com pequeno ordenado, que vive com luxo, se não herdou, furtou. Os cargos do Estado, em mãos de probidade, dão proveito, e honra: em mãos de corrupção, dão proveito sem honra. A probidade do empregado público não pode viver, nem com o luxo, nem com a miséria. Os escritores assalariados, de ordinário, são como as rameiras; prostituem-se a quem lhes paga. Se a honra de representar a nação pela deputação fosse estéril de empregos, e distinções, haveria menos quem a ambicionasse. Aos déspotas nunca faltam mandarins, que sejam vis executores dos seus decretos. Qualquer grumete se reputa habilitado a dirigir o leme da nau do Estado; por isso, ela, muitas vezes, sofre avarias. Um governo sábio deve criar homens para empregos e não empregos para homens. Há honras sem honra, assim como há honra sem honras.*

by subtle juridical interpretations). Willing to eternize themselves in high places: if not here, so, it could be there... None of this is good for their respective republics and says everything about their republican spirit. The positions are to be left on time, or whenever necessary, according either to dignity or to opportunity, or both. Whoever is in office will only be truly free, and therefore truly competent, when he or she is capable of leaving his place without problems, head on without sorrow—even in protest, even to be a candidate again... There are such cases of dignity and honesty. Some retreat just to campaign again at the next election. We have to carefully analyze the context, the reasons, and the ulterior steps of each case.

If there is an authoritarian mentality and avid hunger for power, even far beyond the time (or the expiration date), the Republican mindset should be beyond the availability, without turning away from facing the responsibilities, but with a full and complete detachment from power.

2.4.4 Public Private Thrift and Liberality

Public money should burn your fingers; it should be something only to handle with the greatest care, and not so often and so freely. Public money should be managed rigorously and sparingly, and never from the perspective of the patrimonial state.[28]

However, the "rule" in private management (and in personal finance management) is not to be greedy, and it is even commendable to contribute to the public good. One should not do charity nor allegiance at the expense of the state (this should make strict social justice—and specially the "social state," which is one of the great achievements of Europe and its "social European model"), but only from his or her pocket. It looks good for a public official or officer to be privately liberal. Not in politics, of course, but in the classic sense of liberality...

2.4.5 Simplicity, Frugality, and Personal Restraint

Freedom should not be confused with personal hands-open. Only some Atticism allows you to have the spirit and be free in the world of seduction and deception that is so closely linked with Power. The fewer possessions, honors, pleasures, or political need to live through power, the more people are free to leave office, and not to be constrained by vassals' bounds.

---

[28] See Vélez Rodríguez (2008).

2.4.6 *Constancy, Smart Adaptability, and Consistency*

If on one hand it should rather break than bend in matters of principle, the fact is that there are situations where you have to bend, not break. Especially when it is realized that a change of context has to force a change in attitude. But this may lead to any abuse and treason to principles. It is wise to know when to bend. But it is honorable to understand the moment when only a rupture may save both the face and the soul and the common good, the *res publica*. One has to have a strong sense of the political moment (in a *kayros* way) and never confuse self-interest with public interest. Again, it is a matter of principles, values, and personal virtues.

2.4.7 *Legalism and Intelligent Criticism: Respect for Laws as Guarantors of Freedom*

The Republicans today are not essentially legalistic or normative positivists, although we know that the philosophical essence of many republics in the nineteenth and in the beginning of the twentieth centuries were positivist. But Auguste Comte's theories and the *dura lex sed lex* blind clerks are far way... At least we hope. The problem lies elsewhere. We should remember that legal certainty is the most elemental level of justice itself. While there may be unjust laws (and it depends on the degree of injustice: social injustice is terrible, but for a classic jurist it would be more tolerable, we have to recognize that, than concrete, flagrant injustice, in a case where we have only two or so people in conflict, a particular case *sub judice*[29]) we always have to ask if their application cannot be a lesser evil.

Unfortunately, the world today is full of exceptions to enforcement of the law (and even exceptions to the enforcement of the constitutional law). Before you cry out against unjust laws (and there will always be some) we must ask ourselves about the faithful compliance (or otherwise) of applicable laws. Increasingly, new tyrants (and little tyrants at all levels) consider themselves above the law (many, although dealing with law everyday even don't think about that...). Only the *décor* at the speech is different, and it is amazing how some people seem not to recognize aspects of tyranny in some situations nowadays.

Let us be wise and practical: it is always more possible to succeed because of arguing the law on one's behalf (and the lower the source of law evocated, the better) than appealing to higher clouds of ethereal justice. This reveals, of course, the tendency of our times toward technicality. In a sense it is not an evil. Ideas that are too general may impair accuracy. And before the prevailing subjectivism some moderation is not objectively evil, especially when based on the law. Concrete law, specific law.

[29] See Ferreira da Cunha (2003), pp. 43–70, spec. 57 et sq.

However, before the turpitude of a blatantly unjust law, some people may be tempted to let the world perish, but fight for justice. It is not advisable to destroy the world. But people should really fight for Justice, even *contra legem*. And in that case the situation is not easy... Sometimes, it is not simply a question of opinion articles, demonstrations, and so on. But sometimes even those may be heroic actions, when forbidden by terrorist powers, not in a democratic situation of fair play.

2.5 Contemporary Political Virtues

2.5.1 Vices, Tyrants, and Little Tyrants

The virtues are obviously opposed to vices, or those these. By definition. But a good part of the enemies of the Republic (the term is not used much, but the reality still exists) are not people, but vices. However, political vices such as crime in the system of law are not modeled, nor correspond without further requirements to sins or immoralities. One thing is crime another is immorality, sin, etc. On the other hand, there may be political vices that are not really moral faults in themselves, such as malpractice, disability, ingenuity, etc. Let us quote Montesquieu, always a great authority in these matters, and almost always moderate and prudent (and here he is wise, without any doubt):

> Tous les vices politiques ne sont pas des vices moraux, tous les vices moraux ne sont pas des vices politiques.[30]

The other group of enemies of the Republic are tyrants and little tyrants. For the latter, we must cite a proposal therapy in the *Manual Anti-Tyrants*, published in Brazil,[31] including (in no order, just as illustrations) the following strategies: seek an identity; lose your fear; learn to say 'No'; seek out sense in nonsense; design a pressure group; legislate, legislate, legislate; associate authority with freedom; associate the authority to learn, to build, although in water; appeal to a 'foreign' court; protect the public square garden; do not forget that the real may be invented; that the profane may be sacralised, remembering that the future is also a longing; change certain death into a possible death; relativize; tell a story without an author, read and write, even when impossible; stoically accentuate the silence; look at what is said don't look at what is done; be radical: find the roots; switch in order to remain.

Survival strategies... But do not forget that tyranny lurks around every corner of our slumber. And we must always be prepared to resist. Whether in macropolitics or the micro-, that seems to be getting worse—what happens in the microphysics of

---

[30] Montesquieu (1784), XIX, 11.

[31] Malato (2009).

power is serious and the media doesn't know or doesn't pay attention. To quote again from Montesquieu: "La servitude commence toujours par le sommeil."[32] This idea is not entirely original, though. The British Republican authors from the seventeenth century, whose work Montesquieu reinforced, at least in part, warned of the defection from public life by wealth and luxury and the establishment of an oligarchy of politicians, as the principle of loss of freedom.[33]

2.5.2 Against License: the Virtues of Delicacy, Attention, and Solidarity

Laxity invades us, along with her daughter tyranny. They grow mainly in micro powers where there should be "civil democracy". An attentive force, a calm one, should be gentle and caring. Without ceasing to be strong, forceful, and irreconcilable with the abuses of tyrants and drowsiness of parasitic lax.

It is necessary to show that the Republic has the reason and the force (to recall the slogan or motto of the Republic of Chile, which, however, is alternative—*por la razón o la fuerza*—, which is not so good…). For example, the Republic will only have credibility when its laws are really something to respect. What this implies is an effective and balanced, educated, fair, and prompt police. Democratic and republican police have very few things in common with the police of a dictatorship. An important test to the Republic and democracy is to compare how the police act and how far their behavior is from that of the police during a tyrannical period.

This also implies a more coherent, discrete, fair judicial system, capable of courage and justice in their decisions, above all. This implies a welfare state, which does not leave citizens in situations of misfortune.

And, last but not least, the Republic implies some room for delicacy and not only brutal assertion of leadership (and eagerness by command), often completely empty of ideas and devoid of virtues…

> Oh, how we wish the childlike delicacy of some of Mozart arias. The delicacy of luminous paintings of Flemish painters, a Vermeer, for example. The delicacy of restful bottles of the still lifes of Morandi. In fact, lack the delicacy of adages.[34]

-so says a text of Affonso Romano de Sant'Anna which we would like to quote fully. And then he anticipates the replica, now in a more obviously political level:

> I know you will say, bureaucracy, traffic, wages, police, injustice, corruption and the government will not let us be gentle.—And I do not know? But again I say unto you, let's be delicate. And, if necessary, cruelly delicate.[35]

---

[32] Montesquieu (1748) XIV, 13.

[33] Audier (2004), pp. 23 et sq.

[34] Romano de Sant'anna (2007), pp. 9.

[35] *Idem, Ibidem*, pp. 10.

2.5.3 Against Privilege: the Virtues of Love of Order Rationality, Fairness, and Equity

Persisting privileges, perks, nepotism, and the like (the problem is whether they are many or few, or when discovered they remain unpunished, etc.), you must use reason and fairness to see what the exceptional circumstances are that justified some unequal treatment, and those that are mere favor or privilege. Everything has to be seen in a fair, logical way, with sensitivity: social, historical, cultural, etc.

It is very interesting to look at the different interpretations of some practices, even by ordinary citizens. There is no unanimity, according to empirical studies.[36] What in a certain limit is still acceptable, of course from a certain discrepancy, may denote lack of awareness or civic laxity, or even worse.

2.5.4 Against Abuse of Power and Corruption: the Virtues of Love to Dialog, Pluralism, Transparency, Accuracy, Control, and Separation of Powers

If power corrupts and abuses, we need mechanisms that control power itself: with transparent walls showing the state, forcing the powerful to explain themselves, to respond, to show what they have and how they acquired it. And in all powers, at all levels, there is always a power to control another power. Interdependence and separation of powers are important. And there should be real independence but with interdependence: because a power must be always subject to scrutiny. Checks and balances, power-locking power—there is no other way to have good government in a republican way.

Organs of one person at any level absolutely require strict control done by plural colleges. The efficiency mania that now overwhelms us can never solve a democratic deficit: on the contrary, it worsens that deficit. Many are now forgetting the fact that in civilized societies (macro- or micro-) people don't live by bread alone (although bread is not for everyone in our world), but the satisfaction of participation in government affairs that concern everyone is also important, as are the values of consideration and respect, etc.

Without separation of powers at all levels there will never be a good Republic. Admittedly, this fundamental principle, one of the foundations of modern constitutionalism (entitled as a *conditio sine qua non* for the existence of the Constitution in Art. 16. of the French Declaration of the Rights of Man and of the Citizen) has largely been put in place. But that does not detract from the validity. If there are irreversible legacies of modern constitutionalism, even only the classical demo-liberal one, separation of powers is part of that legacy. And along with it, also those

[36] For the case of Brazil, Almeida and Young (2007), pp. 43 et sq.

basic other features of constitutionalism: the fundamental and human rights, suffrage and representation in power. All of these are republican principles that newcomers ignore or despise. It is a serious problem if young generations really aren't educated in those sacred principles. Too often we hear inconsequential and *blasé* speeches praising the savior, the leader, the dictatorship that they never experienced. Or, worse, some minorities really engage in neo-Nazism and the like. Fascism is a permanent menace to a Europe in crisis.[37]

2.5.5 Against Achilles Complex: Zeno

If there are things that move, and others that are stuck, sometimes one should move, sometimes stand and endure. In our fast-paced life today, it takes being able to run in order to stand in the same place... Republican politics cannot be frozen in the past. It must have enough coherence for the recognition of errors, for example. There are leading principles, but reality is changing, and in many situations it is necessary to act (and think) otherwise. Although coherence always shows itself, even in hard cases—maybe especially in those. Furthermore, the Republic is not one to fall asleep,[38] leaving the field open to dictatorship.

Those pure hands (to remember a sentence from Péguy), who refuse to engage in public affairs, in most cases because of laziness and selfishness, also resolve nothing. Criticizing the very bad politicians, but not daring to oppose them or compete against them. Cicero wrote:

> Those apologies, therefore, in which men take refuge as an excuse for their devoting themselves with more plausibility to mere inactivity do certainly not deserve to be listened to; when, for instance, they tell us that those who meddle with public affairs are generally good-for-nothing men, with whom it is discreditable to be compared, and miserable and dangerous to contend, especially when the multitude is in an excited state. On which account it is not the part of a wise man to take the reins, since he cannot restrain the insane and unregulated movements of the common people. Nor is it becoming to a man of liberal birth, say they, thus to contend with such vile and unrefined antagonists, or to subject one's self to the lashings of contumely, or to put one's self in the way of injuries which ought not to be borne by a wise man. As if to a virtuous, brave, and magnanimous man there could be a juster reason for seeking the government than this–to avoid being subjected to worthless men, and to prevent the Commonwealth from being torn to pieces by them; when, even if they were then desirous to save her, they would not have the power...[39]

---

[37] Riemen (2010).

[38] Montesquieu (1748), XIV, 13.

[39] Cicero, *República*, I, 5. Translation in http://www.gutenberg.org/cache/epub/14988/pg14988.txt.

2.5.6 Against the Wolves and Foxes: Doves–Serpents

It is often said that politicians would be predators: wolves and foxes, with feral cunning, among other figures of the bestiary, either from natural history or from the fantastic. But there is almost a unanimity that there are more truculent treacherous and dangerous politics in other human activities. Anyway, the wisdom of the serpent and the dove's candor should guide the footsteps of republican politicians, neither naïve nor cynical.

2.5.7 Against Corruption and Other Tricks, the Division, the Profusion of "Hats"

In the nineteenth century, electoral frauds were relatively frequent, at least in some countries. In Portugal, they were called "chapeladas" (tricks with a hat), because the extra and fraudulent votes were often cast at the ballot boxes from inside large peasant hats. More recently the ways to steal some money and confuse funds, hide activities, and corrupt the normal control of public accounts are much more subtle. It is, in all cases, the old patrimonial state behavior. The power of a few is therefore to get votes that will give a face to formal legitimacy. But how do people do that? No longer with large hats full of false votes, in principle. The new means are marketing, propaganda, media control, public, or private. These methods are used around the word and assert an important role in influencing consciences and votes.

Even leaders, bosses, employees at a certain level of power, good fathers, and good mothers, full of hard work and at least some sense of justice too, very often with good intentions and goodwill, even those, who are far from the profile of the tyrant or dictator, even these, we insist, sometimes cannot separate the public from the private, public finance from private: they mix up what it is to be a representative, or employee, or the face of a company, and what is to be Mr or Mrs X or Y, the simple citizen, a private person: and it is a very perverse confusion.

The difficulty of distinguishing functions when acting in private (even if to be boss, or manager, or foreman functions are not strictly private, but social—and even symbolic) is immense. The right pocket of the boss is not the public and the left one the private… We need more separation… of pockets.

This form of governing, managing, and living in society cannot continue. It is profoundly monarchical. How important were the stewards of kings! Public debt and debt to personal suppliers of the king, like tailors and so on, took time to separate. And this cut is always a big problem for democracy. We hear so many stories about public services and public possessions used by rulers, even in democracy, in their own private interest (not only cars, aeroplanes, secretaries…). No smoke without fire—people say. The issue, anyhow, is more complex than a simple historical dimension (or family one). And results of this confusion (not a naive one) is serious injury for the social whole.

There are many minor attitudes in the holders of power, mostly small but decisive, which show the greatest confusion and even promiscuity. We should separate between the hats we use in public and in private. And who, in a simple letter, petition, or public intervention addresses some authority by 'Your Excellency' cannot finish that with 'kisses' or 'hugs,' even if in private life they are close friends or relatives. The best would be that people close to the petitioners would never decide on those petitions. And of course official documents should never be addressed to the name of the person who is, at the moment, holding the position. That is a way of making it personal again. The problem is that in many services, private and even public, those who depend on the top think that if they do not use the name of their master they won't be cared for. Sometimes they even fear not to be heard if they don't perform all the submissive rituals… And naming the "master" is considered in some places to be one of the rules.

One of the great losses of our society was the sense of *nuances*, both useful for faster and smooth social relations, how to show displeasure, social avoidance, bitterness, or covering someone with ridicule (as in the film *Ridicule*, significantly depicting the court of France in their last days immediately before the outbreak of the Revolution) and so on. The famous letter[40] from Pina Manique, dated 22 October 1795, while Chief Justice of Santarém to the Duke of Cadaval in which he was addressed by "thou" (*Du* in German, *Tu* in French, Portuguese and other Latin languages) is of course an excess of self-defense, but there is no doubt that he was covered by reason. Even a Minister cannot treat a Chief Justice in a Latin country by the colloquial and familiar formula, even being a Duke.

Some will tell us that we are surrendering to an aristocratic logic. By no means. The aristocratic vision of the world has no monopoly on order, hierarchy, and education; on the contrary. It is no easy matter to know whether a rational order such as the one that aspires to establish the Republic could someday do without the aid of symbols and rituals and speak more directly to sensitivity and intuition, eventually reach people more easily: which are, on a superficial level, less speculative, less rational, etc.

It seems to us that some care is needed to not fall into hyper-rationalism, the geometric mania of abstract utopias, which can be manufactured with the underworld dreams of less sensitive men. Along with freedom, some democratic order, hierarchy, and above all, respect is needed. Respect is the other name (and the counterpart) of dignity. Not the 'very beautiful little respect' (a sentence often used in Portuguese Salazar's dictatorship, often said with a hypocritical musicality, to mean the need for obedience without any discussion) infused with fear (or, in some cases, even among educated and cultured people, the famous 'reverential fear'), but the respect due to the appreciation, recognition of the value and functions of others, and the respect that all human beings fully deserve.

---

[40] See Maranhão Filho (2008), pp. 47–50. Online: http://lildbi.bireme.br/lildbi/docsonline/lilacs/20090300/150-LILACS-UPLOAD.pdf.

A great drama of the younger generations (and not so young…), thankfully not all, is the inability to admire institutions and people. Their often fleeting heroes are catwalk models who do not speak, singers and actors who did not write what they say: and not always the best of the latter, nor the most beautiful of the former. It is a very bad sign to see that even intelligent young people fulfilling their academic obligations, dislike the University, and in many cases do not even know the names of their own professors. Some finish their courses without having bought a single book. And not all of those few who did really opened them.

Admiration was once an academic reality. Masters had disciples; even if there was sometimes a mixture of admiration with a kind of Oedipus' complex, and the secret (or not so secret) desire of the "death of the Father," as in the paradigmatic case of Freud. But today it seems that there are no more disciples… and there are no more masters without them… It is the disciple that makes the master, because he or she chooses him or her. There is no other way.

Although this subject is not of prime importance, it is certain that a society in which intelligence is not organized and harmonious and there is no veneration and respect, is a community with memory deficits that will lead to future deficits too.

But even worse is the infantilism and contempt of youth culture (fuelled by powerful consumption machines). Everything sees young people in a never-ending minority, the precise opposite of Enlightenment as Kant underlined.

It would be a disaster if the culture of mere leisure might invade schools and the pursuit of serious study: the world of labor. The hedonist simply can never be a really good student (although the laxity of our education gives approbation easily, and sometimes good grades without too much effort or capacity). Therefore it is recommended that young people use at least two hats: the hat for work and the hat for leisure. And those who exercise power are urged to wear many hats according to each position they occupy. And please do not mix hats and positions: each position needs a special and proper hat.

2.5.8 Against Ignorance, Obscurantism, Apathy, Servility, Inhumanity, Lack of Direction: the Love for Culture and Education; and the Education for Citizenship and Human Rights

The triumphant time of the Enlightenment and its audacious promises is too far now. Evidently elites, certain elites continue to be faithful to the same values and virtues. We cannot forget that, as Kant put it in his *Was ist Aufklärung?* Enlightenment was the way out of servitude for Mankind, the possibility of attaining majority. But mass society,[41] rampant consumerism, the demagoguery of many

[41] See Ehrhardt Soares (2008).

politicians, the flattery of the voters, the 'compulsory un-education' with the necessary drawdown (despite the prodigious and admirable opening opportunities), association with drugs and organized crime, etc., all this and more puts large sections of the world population further from those high standards. To a large extent world civilization is in retreat. Oddly enough, our societies are very tribal. They lack true dialog (not monologs juxtaposed between the deaf) and, of course, consensus. Consensus based on differences, not on *unanimism*. We are getting very extreme societies, clenched. The moderates[42] are viewed askance. Everything has to be black or white. "So then because thou art lukewarm, and neither cold nor hot, I will spue thee out of my mouth"—says the Apocalypse.[43] But sometimes things are subtle and mixed up: it cannot be all hot or all cold… People also speak too much about the end of the world. But the real problem is the other: the possibility of the end of the European world, "as we know it", as we are used to.

Someone also said that societies are of value because of the radicals, but only preserved by moderates. And moderation—it should be noted—does not mean tepid hesitations.

The demagogue might take account of public opinion, and, above all, opinion that is published. There is a glaring lack of a sense of humor, subtlety, and irony. People often forget who the "main enemy" is. They give shots in all directions and some shots in their own feet. Some political actors have specialized in it and become very competent.

Many media are increasingly sensationalist. And many are looking for scapegoats. Their need for constant *new* sensational news obliges many to sacrifice truth, honesty, rigor. The circus (circus and blood—*panem et circensis*—is first and foremost) is there to feed the masses who are more and more hypnotized, but sometimes beginning to ask themselves where this is taking them. *The show must go on*… And they must not awake from the dream… even if it is becoming a nightmare.

But things are getting worse. And it is becoming stylish (for the moment in marginal circles, fortunately: but it is increasing in more and more social circles) not to be a Democrat, not to share fundamental values, which, in summary, are those of the Universal Declaration of Human Rights. Already some say it is the fault of parties, or MPs, this or that group… There are easy targets, traditional ones… European discontent may turn against the normal political actors, both from the right wing and the left wing: and the possibility of emerging authoritarian or even totalitarian leaders is not a vain possibility. We only have to watch the signs and how History may repeat its errors and terrors.

The Democrats and Republicans (in European terms, not specifically the two main USA parties) have a duty to defend the institutions, to justify the work of parliaments (particularly vulnerable to ignorant mass: they are easy prey to populism—but obviously parliaments, at least in some countries, need to improve their

---

[42] Also it occurred in the times of Bonnard (1936).

[43] Ap. III, 16.

composition and their work), as a defensive shield for minorities who can be slaughtered by the vandalism of the repressed, the ill-informed, and also those whose only power is a protest vote in any referendum.

We've been too distracted, but "they are there again." We need to take the utmost care with Manichaeism. Beware of demagoguery. And greater attention given to internal divisions among Democrats, bickering among brothers, the democratic parties which are so often smaller and out of power, "groups of friends who hate each other cordially." Divisions can and do exist naturally in pluralism. But there are divisions and different ways which only carry water to the mill of those who like a faceless unanimity: and only the face of those people would be just the face of the dictator. In essence, what is at stake is the atavistic appeal for order, obedience, even without freedom, always convenient for spirits who are not free. And it's anything inherent to monarchical spirit, as Alain already suspected:

> La monarchie semble donc être une partie de l'ordre. (…) ceux qui célèbrent l'ordre, le pouvoir fort, et l'obéissance, disent des choses évidentes et que tout le monde sait.[44]

Everyone understands the language of force. Freedom is much more difficult to understand.

We know it is also a quality problem: when bureaucratic politicians segregated by party machines and the "elites" that the media creates reveal abysses of training and intelligence among themselves, it seems to us very natural that some people will truly irritate some others.

We still have to defend democracy more effectively and assertively. Democrats and Republicans must be prepared: just read in the stars of social unrest… the anti-democratic and anti-republican few are now reviling again who they are and what they want. These are a growing, not strictly marginal, phenomena. Not, of course, at least for the moment, as a real danger in a general election—that would be a certain contradiction in terms of their existence, although not completely original. The anti-Democrats and those who do not want the Republic are few by nature, but they can drag many in some crucial moments of crisis. Those in favor of democracy have to stop the inconsistent triumphalism of the republics (and curiously also its low profile) and should think of defending themselves. First, giving the least warned citizen reasons to love and to defend democracy and the republic. This would be the best antidote. The problem is that common people, and youth do not see the benefits of the *statu quo*. And some may be seduced even by the idea that dictatorship is best.

The institutional integration in Europe is still a barrier against greater temptations, especially in South European countries. But for how long, if they are massacred by an austerity from which that they don't see any benefit, even in the long term, an austerity with moral labelling and many attacks on peoples' dignity? Even the label PIGS or PIIGS is, of course, against the dignity of those countries. And the sensationalism of some "media" doesn't help.

[44] Alain (1962), pp. 213.

If we read carefully many of the comments on current political news on the Internet we certainly begin to understand. Whoever has the stomach, please read two or three at random. So much poison, so much hatred. We see two possible reasons for that: either there are groups determined to sink the morale of some countries, and propagate these posts of anger, impropriety, discontent, even outrage, systematically, or else there are worrying slices of the population… that may not even vote, but weigh in social unrest. Because what they say in the blogosphere they also would say on the street, among their friends and relatives, in the market, in the place of employment…

There is a lot of work to do, taking care of educating future elites. Only Democratic and Republican elites may protect the mass from oligarchies. Unfortunately, not too many people understand that, living in the confusion of a base centered and beheaded "democracy" with real democracy, which implies, at least since Aristotle, a mixed government.

Unlike some, with no ethics and no shame, we believe that a teacher has a duty (without hypocrisy to pretend being aseptic) to maintain independence and not make any kind of indoctrination or proselytizing among their students. But societies cannot get though the Republic disarmed ideologically especially when the growing nostalgia is out there. Our young have been born after the reestablishment of democracy in all the Western European countries, and have no patterns for comparison. With the general lack of culture and history that our schools insist on perpetuating, by passivity and excess of teaching technicalities at the expense of training most things get worse: because young people are occupied, but not with the City's most basic problems. Also at this level, the "back to the basics" is a good motto. If basics are really basics, of course.

Then where are the youth organizations of the democratic parties? And also the young Democrats and Republicans without party affiliation. They are needed. They are indispensable to defend our past conquests and to build the future. But too many people say that they only care about new posts in the state administration. An answer to that must be remembered: "No jobs for the boys."[45]

Curious ingenuity according to which, having achieved democracy (and still imperfect, technical, super-structural) and the Republic, there will be no more dangers to democracy and to the Republic! There will be a weariness of Democrats and Republicans, or their complacency, perhaps because of the general lack of historical culture. And what about the lack of civic education and human rights?

If we look at what seems to be sleepwalking punctuated with peaks of frenzy and despair, early disease and even death,[46] many young people in our so-called societies "of abundance," certainly recognize, first of all, the meaningless of life, the emptiness of existence. Naturally powered by idleness and lax families through education (no time for the young, no time to educate, and also—even worse—no values for both), but also by the lack of targets (the generalized "no job" ideology is

---

[45] See the history of this topic in Malato and Ferreira da Cunha (2007), pp. 287.

[46] Kierkegaard (1849).

very dangerous—but the fault is on the policies that imply cuts and more cuts, thereby increasing unemployment to unimaginable rates).

Many opinion makers present our times as if we live immersed in corruption. To be fair, honesty and industry seem to be outdated, at least for those who have ambition. This ambience cannot inculcate anything positive in the young generations. Of course that is required to relentlessly fight the wounds that undermine the health of the Republic, erode confidence, and give the worst examples. But beyond that task, belonging mainly to those who have specific responsibilities in this matter, at the State level, there is upstream work that can only result from a vehement change of attitude toward education on the part of State. A fight against Ignorance, Obscurantism, Apathy, leading of course to claim everything from the State, with a concomitant perversion of welfare that endangers the essential welfare state and the extinction of resources that should be used for the truly needy. And yet, those who do not know, who do not cherish, who have no occupation, who have no dignity—decay in servility, can even slip into the meshes of marginality, or the false salvations of Fundamentalism, Terrorism, etc. Only a pure love for culture and education (and Education for Citizenship and Human Rights) by the Republicans (and all people of good will) can still avoid the cultural and spiritual impoverishment of the people of Southern Europe, of nothing good for the Republic and a real danger to all Europe. Because the fascist phenomena that it may bring are of course contagious, and the suspension of the Constitution in a single European poor country may give bad ideas to many people in other rich European societies.

Large masses who are truly uneducated, although formally educated in schools and universities, endowed with many degrees, people tuned by the commonplace of television (in the best case, the simple sensationalist news), trained to pay attention for the time that an ad on television lasts, are the kind of people demagogic dictators need. Too many citizens are conditioned by propaganda, and even more so by its intrinsic limitations of culture, education, and critical thinking.

The Republic is first and foremost an ethic. But this ethic is only able to flourish with citizens who are able to understand and put it into practice in their lives. This is not possible with citizen-servants, narcotized citizens, or even people so desperate in the struggle for survival at the material level (or fever for accumulating more material possessions: there is slavery on both sides…). Those somnambular people have no time for the *agora*, and the time that it necessarily consumes, and not always with immediate results.

Philosophy, Thought, Culture, require a material base that sustains the necessary leisure (leisure with dignity, as stated Seneca—not "idleness, the mother of all vices"). Everybody knows (or should know) this historically, from Ancient Greece, the mother of Democracy and the Republic. How can we not think about it now?

It is not worth crying for ethics and the Republic if there is not enough wealth and fair distribution of this wealth, and at the same time enough lucidity not to get into a whirlwind of work and endless consumption. When the main and perhaps only purpose of life is the material, through starvation or greed, values are things of the mind, and virtues that are values in action have no way to survive.

And so, in the Republic, change starts from within, with the change of mentalities and life goals. But also consider the air of the times. And the illustrious and enlightened thinkers of ancient times, the Republicans, as their spiritual grandchildren, believe that the only way out is education: in the family, at school, in the media.

References

Alain (1962). *Politique*. Paris: PUF.

Almeida, A. C., & Young, C. (2007). Corrupção: Com jeitinho parece que vai. In A. Cabeça (Ed.), *do Brasileiro* (2nd ed.). Rio de Janeiro: Record.

Audier, S. (2004). *Les Théories de la République*. Paris: La Découverte.

Bittar, E. C. B. (2005). *O Direito na Pós-Modernidade*. Rio de Janeiro: Forense.

Bonnard, A. (1936). *Les modérés*. Paris: Grasset.

Calvino, I. (2002). *Lezioni Americane, Sei proposte per il prossimo Milenio*. 4th ed. Port. transl. by J.C. Barreiros. *Seis Propostas para o Próximo Milénio*. Lisboa: Teorema.

Chamon Junior, L. A. (2007). *Teoria Geral do Direito Moderno. Por uma Reconstrução Crítico-Discrusiva na Alta Modernidade* (2nd ed.). Rio de Janeiro: Lumen Juris.

Cicero, *República*, I, 5. Translation in http://www.gutenberg.org/cache/epub/14988/pg14988.txt.

Cotterrell, R. (2003). *The Politics of Jurisprudence* (2nd ed.). Oxford and New York: Oxford University Press.

de Castro Osório, A. (2008). *A Minha Pátria* (new ed.). Sintra: Colares Editora.

Débord, G. (1940/2007). *La société du spectacle*. Translated by E. dos Santos Abreu, *A Sociedade do Espectáculo*. Rio de Janeiro: Contraponto, 9.a reimp.

Dembour, M.-B. (1990). Le pluralisme juridique: une démarche parmi d'autres, et non plus innocente. *Revue Interdisciplinaire d'Etudes Juridiques*, 24, 43 et sq.

Douzinas, C., & Gearey, A. (2005). *Critical Jurisprudence. The Political Philosophy of Justice*. Oxford and Portland: Hart.

Ehrhardt Soares, R. (2008). *Direito Público e Sociedade Técnica* (2nd ed.). Coimbra: Atlântida.

Faria Costa, J. F. de (1993). *O Direito*, Porto: *a Fragmentaridade e o Nosso Tempo*.

Ferreira da Cunha, P. (2009). *Pensar o Estado*. Lisboa: Quid Juris.

Ferreira da Cunha, P. (2003). As Duas Justiças—Justiça Moral e Política *vs*. Justiça Jurídica (A partir do Comentário de Tomás de Aquino ao Livro V da Ética a Nicómaco de Aristóteles). In: P. Ferreira da Cunha (Ed.), *O Século de Antígona*. Coimbra, Almedina.

Ferreira da Cunha, P. (1991). *Pensar o Direito*. Almedina: II. Da Modernidade à Postmodernidade. Coimbra.

Filho, M. (2008). Carta de Pina Manique: tourettismo, desabafo sarcástico ou folclore? Nota Histórica. *Revista Brasileira de Neurologia*, 44(2), 47–50. http://lildbi.bireme.br/lildbi/docsonline/lilacs/20090300/150-LILACS-UPLOAD.pdf.

Finkielkraut, A. (2009). *Un coeur intelligent. Lectures*. Paris: Stock/Flammarion.

Finley, M. I. (1976). *Démocratie antique et démocratie modern*. Trad. by M. Alexandre, preceded of *Tradition de la démocracie grecque,* P. Vidal-Naquet. Paris: Payot.

Jones, A. H. M. (1986). *Athenian Democracy*. Baltimore: The Johns Hopkins University Press.

Kierkegaard, S. (1849). *Sygdommen til Døden* (under the pseudonym of Anti-Climacus).

Livy (Titus Livius Patavinus), *Ab Urbe Condita.*

Malato, M. L. (2009). *Manual Anti-Tiranos. Retórica, Poder e Literatura*. Porto Alegre: Livraria do Advogado Editora.

Malato, M. L., & Ferreira da Cunha, P. (2007). *Manual de Retórica e Direito*. Lisbon: Quid Juris.

Maltez, J. A. *blog Sobre o Tempo que Passa.* http://tempoquepassa.blogspot.com/.

Matyszak, P., & Berry, J. (2008). *Lives of the Romans*. London: Thames & Hudson.

Montesquieu (1748). *De l'Esprit des Lois.*

Morais de Carvalho, A. A. (1850). *Aphorismos e Pensamentos Moraes, Religiosos*. Lisbon: *Politicos e Philosophicos*.

Morrison, W. (1997). *Jurisprudence: From the Greeks to Post-Modernism*. London: Cavendish.

Mossé, C. (1993). *Le Citoyen dans la Grèce Antique*. Paris: Nathan.

Palmer, R. R. (1963). Notes on the Use of the Word "Democracy"., *Political Science Quarterly*, 68, 1789–1799.

Pereira Marques, F. (2002). *Esboço de um Programa para os Trabalhos das Novas Gerações*. Porto: Campo das Letras.

Puy, F. (1993). *La Socialdemocracia y su Parentela Ideológica*, "Anuario del Filosofia del Derecho", Nova época, tomo X, Madrid.

Quinet, E. (2009). *La République. Conditions de la régénération de la France, présentation de Juliette Grange*. Paris and Sofia: Le Bord de L'eau.

Raaflaub, K. A., et al. (2007). *Origins of democracy in ancient Greece*. Berkeley: University of California Press.

Riemen, R. (2010). *De eeuwige terugkeer van het fascism*. Amsterdam: Uitgeverij Atlas.

Rocha Pereira, M. H. da (1980). *Estudos de História da Cultura Clássica, Cultura Grega*, Lisbon: Fundação Calouste Gulbenkian, 1(5).

Rojas, E. (1994). *O Homem Light*. Gráfica de Coimbra: Uma Vida sem Valores. Translated by V.M. Neves. Coimbra.

Romano de Sant'anna, A. (2007). *Tempo de Delicadeza*. Porto Alegre: L&PM.

Rousseau, J.-J. (1764/1782-1789). *Lettres écrites de la montagne*. Edition Du Peyrou/Moultou. electronic ed. http://ftp.ac-toulouse.fr/pub/philosophie/rousseaulettresecritesdelamontagne.rtf-.

Sansot, P. (2000). *Du bon usage de la lenteur*. Paris: Payot/Rivages.

Thorley, J. (2004). *Athenian Democracy* (2nd ed.). London and New York: Routledge.

Vallançon, F. (1989). Images romaines de morale et de droit. Devotio et fides. *Archives de Philosophie du Droit*, XXXIV, 304–333.

Vélez Rodríguez, R. (2008). *A Análise do Patrimonialismo através da Literatura Latino-Americana. O Estado gerido como bem familiar*. Rio de Janeiro: Documenta Histórica Editora/ Instituto Liberal.

Vidal-Naquet, P. (2002). *Les Grecs, les historiens, la démocratie: le grand écart*, portuguese translation by J. Batista Neto, *Os Gregos, os Historiadores e a Democracia: O grande desvio*. São Paulo: Companhia das Letras.

Villey, M. (1982). *Précis de Philosophie du Droit, I* (3rd ed.). Paris: Dalloz.

Ward, I. (2004). *Introduction to critical legal theory* (2nd ed.). Milton Park and New York: Routledge-Cavendish.

Zambrano, M. (1993). La Metáfora del Corazón. In: J. Moreno Sanz (Ed.), *La Razón en la Sombra, Antologia del Pensamiento de María Zambrano,* p. 108 et sq.

Chapter 3
Political Values

> (...) *se constituye en un Estado social y democrático de Derecho, que propugna como valores superiores de su ordenamiento jurídico la libertad, la justicia, la igualdad y el pluralismo político.*
>
> Spanish Constitution, Article 1

3.1 Republic: An Axiological Topic

> (...) to institute a Democratic State for the purpose of ensuring the exercise of social and individual rights, liberty, security, well being, development, equality and justice as supreme values of a fraternal, pluralist and unprejudiced society, based on social harmony and committed, in the internal and international spheres, to the peaceful solution of disputes (...)
>
> Preamble of the Brazilian Constitution[1]

We began the republican values' investigation without a classical ode to the triad "Freedom, Equality, and Fraternity," not for its minor importance (it summarizes vectors of the human spirit that we have not been able to accomplish yet and which remain as some of the greatest desires of enlightened humanity), but because they keep on developing, articulating, and materializing in multiple axiological topics, of which the Preamble of the Brazilian Constitution is one of the most eloquent examples.[2] With the advantage of articulating and balancing all the values, principles and rights that nowadays compete for a renewed idea of Republic.

Nowadays, it is necessary, of course, not to consider the values in abstract (even without naming them) but, on the other hand, to think them over and to practice them in comparison with other alternative values and with the respective anti-values.

In a very inspirational conference on the present and the past of the Republic, the historian António Reis asks: "What are, then, the republican values? How are they distinguished from the liberal values, the conservative values and the socialists'

---

[1] *Apud* http://web.mit.edu/12.000/www/m2006/teams/willr3/const.htm.

[2] For more developments, see Ferreira da Cunha (2009a), pp. 94 et sq.

P. Ferreira da Cunha, *Political Ethics and European Constitution*,
SpringerBriefs in Law, DOI 10.1007/978-3-662-45600-2_3

values? Why the need to talk today of the republic values again, when Europe has lived the second half of the twentieth century immersed in the confrontation between a liberal-conservative ideology, the socialist-democratic ideology and the communist ideology?"[3]

And the conclusions that we come up with are fully satisfying. Whether it is about the values that keep on enunciating affirmatively, or whether it is about what concerns the enemies of those values.

3.2 Idea of Republic

The first axiological idea we have in this matter, although it is not in itself only a value, is the idea of *Republic.* Already in Rome, after a complex evolution, the *Res Publica* was seen with respect, veneration, even dedication. Because the *public thing* is a thing of everyone, it is above of the individualisms (and particularisms and egoisms).

Republican ethics are opposed in a way, to the kingdom's mythification, which can as well, naturally, have mythical ethical elements.

Simply put, apart from some cases the monarchical ethic refers above all, to great deeds and great designs, in many cases divines (*in hoc signo vinces* is a sign to the victory of not only one imperial or monarchic ruler in Europe, etc.), preferring emotion to reason. So, reason, public utility, the good of the greatest number and common efforts are primary elements to have in the public republican ethic.

3.3 State, Democracy, and Human Rights

Although republicanism is moderate and opting clearly for the public interest, it does not stop from being attentive to the needs and rights of the people. Being aware of the importance of the State, republicans are not friends of State hypertrophy: nor the minimal state, nor the monstrous state, but the optimal one. They are defenders of a State (better said, of the Republic, but that would be a detail for now) educator and communicator, fully democratic (with suffrage, representativeness, political pluralism, etc.), and Human Rights paladins.

Ultraliberalism (at least the ultraliberal or neoliberal canon, because there are many liberalisms), by the extreme emphasizing of the individual does not match the ethical republican's ideals, which are not individualistic and more social than collective (but never collectivists). Although, surely, the class particularism of the socialisms (and they are equally plural) also does not instigate republican applause, which would stay in a position between the liberal and the socialist, or better. Being able to raise, whether in liberals as well as in socialists, that moderation and

[3] Reis (2002), pp. 11–12.

deliberation of contraries that balance freedom with equality, in a way that hopefully may one day lead to the bloom of the fraternity.

These ideals evidently have shades. Denis Collin, for example, finishes his book-manifest "Revive la République," in a way which is not very divergent, but has other tones. He suggests an alternative:

> (…) si nous voulons sauvegarder non seulement l'héritage du mouvement ouvrier, mais aussi le meilleur de notre passé républicain et le meilleur de la tradition libérale.[4]

Evidently, strictly speaking, neither the State, nor the democracy in its diverse manifestations, even Human Rights are not valued. They all seem to be inserted in the extent of a greater value, which is Freedom, but a more consequential and complete Freedom than the classical one.

3.4 Political Values and Axiological Topics

Truthfully, the republican values (or, if we prefer, the republican superior values—since there might be others which are subordinate to them: sometimes called principles) are those from the well-known triad: Freedom, Equality, and Fraternity. As superior values, or secondary values, or—we believe that it's even better—principles, arising from these values are secularism and citizenship.

The case of Justice is more complex: it is, without doubt, a superior value but not only republican, being sometimes put in the place of Fraternity (such as in the Spanish Constitution) for several reasons, but in general, sort of announcing it. As a species of transitory value (but not less important because of that), it's not overcome in its full realization, the Fraternity. Justice is not only a value, but also a juridical principle.

Let us pay a little attention afterward to two "secondary" values, or principles more currently invoked. We believe that secularism is a specification of the two first values. Implying, right away, full religious freedom, positive, negative, and neutral, as well as neutrality and equality in the treatment of all. Another value of this kind is citizenship: It is especially an implementation of freedom, as well as political pluralism.

The importance of talking of "values" (*improprio* sensu) such as democracy, human rights, political pluralism, secularism, or citizenship is calling attention to the faces that assume the revolutionary values of Freedom, Equality, and Fraternity today, in the concrete of the political fight. So, not as values, but as valorative topics, they are of great importance.

[4] Denis (2005), p. 226 ("(…) if we want to save not only the heritage of the labour movement, but also the best of our republican past and the best of the liberal tradition (…)").

3.5 Enemies of the Republic and Their Antidotes

Politics is always, at least partly, opposition between friend and enemy (*Freund/ Feind*). That is why certain authors (some surely less republican) invented it. And the Republic goes wrong if, wrapped in its idealism, it forgets the elementary truths of politics.

The Republic cannot be kept from bothering those that do not affiliate with their point of view, the ones that are or would be impaired materially or in immaterial privileges with their full realization, etc. For that (or because of that), there are people who do not like it, and people who fight against it. And nothing would be more natural. What we should never have is a Manichean attitude, according to which "who isn't for us is against us." The republican idea has already suffered, in some cases, from an exaggerated fervor that mistreated and even suppressed the enemies. It is not the case in any way nowadays, in which it has learned its lessons. So, by talking about "Republic enemies," we are not even talking about concrete people. But about positions, perspectives and realities that counter it.

Contemporary society has a few enemies of the Republic. But there is no invincible enemy, because in it is the force to win, or to go on winning. We should not think that there is, as in the *International* verse, a "final struggle." The struggle against obscurantism, privilege, and prejudice is part of everyday struggle. And when we hoped the struggle had been won, once again the stone rolls to the foot of the mountain of History, so the republican Sisyphus goes back to the struggle, to the climbing.

António Reis, in the aforementioned conference, enunciates not enemies, but dangers to the republican values. It is important to quote:

> The education for citizenship is just as urgent as we know the dangers that threaten republican values. Without being exhaustive, we shall enumerate some of them:
>
> 1. The culture of the egotist individualism and of the values of the personal success, of easy money, in clear opposition to the communitarian feeling of 'res publica' and to the individual sense of honour and merit for work.
> 2. Corporatism, lobbyism and populism, in opposition to the culture of national and public interest.
> 3. Laxity, in opposition to the courageous democratic authority.
> 4. The devaluation of the culture of public service and of the role of the State, with the negative consequences that that diminishes the value of equality and justice.
> 5. The cultural homogenization of globalisation, with the threat to national cultural identity.
> 6. Xenophobia and racism, in opposition to the universal sense of Humanity.
> 7. The indifference or even contempt by politics and politicians, with the concurrent elevation of economics, in opposition to participative citizenship.
> 8. The pseudo democracy of opinion or television democracy, with privilege granted to spontaneous and individual opinion, through polls or statements, easily confused with the totality of the opinion, and which ignores the need for mediation of organized

> participation in institutions, harming the debate, personal reflection and the exercise of a critical spirit (…)"[5]

From these topics it is not hard to enunciate the necessary antidotes in summary, some of which could really be based on the respective roman values:

(a) *Honor et Labor.* Honor and merit for work—*dignitas, industria…*
(b) *Patria, Res Publica*—culture of public and national interest, that reinforces the national cultural identity, with a culture of public service and of State.
(c) *Firmitas*—democratic authority—not only *auctoritas*, but an actuating *potestas,* bound to *auctoritas*.
(d) A bit less Roman, certainly, are the important and necessary axiological topics of *Universalism*, of *participative Citizenship*[6] and of the *Democracy, non-populist and non-depending on media.*

All these vectors need to be framed and promoted for an education for citizenship, for Human Rights, and in fact an extended legal education, not to make citizens obedient to the laws (no one obeys from only knowing), but above all to make them conscious of the rights and duties and of their close interconnection. Authors like Norberto Bobbio have already realized that the democracy could pay the price for not educating (sufficiently, properly).

Republican ideas do not agree with institutional and legal laxity, nor with neoliberal dismantlement of the State, instead they want a vigorous State (though flexible and naturally democratic, of rights and of culture), capable of assuming the fullness of its functions, all of its functions. And one of the essential tools of that renewal of the State (non statist, non totalitarian nor collectivist—obviously) is precisely the explanation of its importance for education. Without it, a passive mentality grows, for which the State, just like Sartre's hell, "it's the others," in relation to who and to whom affinity and duties are not recognized. This mentality leads to parasitism that always calls for subsidies and handouts from the State, without giving anything in return. And it is this parasitism that set at risk—caricatured and made gigantic by the market theologians, betting on the dismantlement of the State and averse to all social policies—the social State.[7]

We end this question by considering what remedies could make the republican citizen flourish, instead of the skills of some and of the cadaveric rigidity of others. Here then, is a text for deep meditation:

> (…) any general organization that limits the individual liberties immediately produces a moving reaction in which everyone is solidary. (…) The police, as representative of the general law, are considered the enemy, therefore reaction appears.

[5] Idem, Ibid, p. 28.

[6] See, however, v.g., Sherwin-White (2001).

[7] About the Social State and the Social Constitution, v. for all, Ferreira da Cunha (2009a), pp. 55 et sq.

In the same way, the official, even when he wears the uniform and is forced to obey the law, has the similar difficulty in representing an impersonal role. (...) The minor official holds desperately to the law, without trying to understand its spirit. He doesn't want to solve any case which is not current and passes it on to his hierarchical superior. He feels bad and uncomfortable, stuck in a straitjacket that stops him from being himself and from supporting his human instinct. (...) This tendency of overlapping the human sympathy to the general requirements of the law means that much of the time, social and public life revolves around the efforts and requests of friends. He is asked to help them pass exams in order to avoid military service, to get a job, to win a case, to pass through life's difficulties (...).[8]

This was typical of Portuguese society in times of the dictatorship. The question is: Was it only in that society and only at that historical period?

3.6 The Way of the Enlightenment and Republican Hope

We live and we will always live in the French Revolution, of the verb of its tribunes, of the thoughts of its philosophers, whose theses, principles, ideas and values will never perish and are constantly renewed, because they unswervingly conjugate two legitimacies, two sovereign wills: one of the People and one of the Nation.

That Revolution progressed like that until the present day, with the social State candied in the principles of freedom, equality and fraternity.

Paulo Bonavides, *Do Estado Liberal ao Estado Social*, 7th ed., 2nd print, São Paulo, Malheiros Editores, 2004, p. 36[9]

It is not convenient to make long considerations about values that are myths, and whose capacity of arousing action and of inspiring fables resides in subliminal appeal, in its immense capacity for acquiring new perceptions and of continuing to bear the same flag for diverse causes. Over the centuries, what Freedom, Equality, Justice, and Fraternity are has been discovered and aggregated into new understanding. At times, correcting others ... here and there proscribing an abusive, local, and particular interpretation. Following a path of rationality, in scope and also attention to the rights of the minorities ... It is an exciting walk that honors Humanity. In a short time (in few centuries, in some cases in a couple of them), the semantic evolution has been a witness of the spirit's progress of humanity in discovering the deepest of its Humanity.

Therefore, it is important to recall the essential milestone that was the proclamation of Humanity's emancipation, with the Enlightenment (that lately has

---

[8] Dias (1985).

[9] Portuguese original: "Nós vivemos e viveremos sempre da Revolução Francesa, do verbo dos seus tribunos, do pensamento de seus filósofos, cujas teses, princípios, ideias e valores jamais pereceram e constantemente se renovam, porquanto conjugam, inarredáveis, duas legitimidades, duas vontades soberanas: a do Povo e a da Nação.

Aquela Revolução prossegue, assim, até chegar aos nossos dias, com o Estado social cristalizado nos princípios da liberdade, igualdade e fraternidade.

had an interesting translation as "clarification"—which it is as well) that made Men begin to shake off (without doubt with not always good attempts) of the minority's shackles.[10] This theoretical proclamation was made, as we know, through Emanuel Kant, in his famous *Was ist Aufklärung*?, in 1783. There's always some desire to read it out loud, as a proclamation of the emancipation that it is:

> Aufklärung ist der Ausgang des Menschen aus seiner selbstverschuldeten Unmündigkeit. Unmündigkeit ist das Unvermögen, sich seines Verstandes ohne Leitung eines anderen zu bedienen. S e l b s t v e r s c h u l d e t ist diese Unmündigkeit, wenn die Ursache derselben nicht am Mangel des Verstandes, sondern der Entschließung und des Mutes liegt, sich seiner ohne Leitung eines andern zu bedienen. Sapere aude! Habe Mut, dich deines e i g e n e n Verstandes zu bedienen ! ist also der Wahlspruch der Aufklärung.[11]

As we know, Republicanism owes a lot to the Enlightenment.[12] As does the French Revolution. Always, as we know, with the shadows that implementation places in the light of ideals. No doubt, Republicanism and Enlightenment are a mark without which Humanity would still live spectrally, with little hope of emancipation. If *Was ist Aufklärung*, by Kant, was the shout for emancipation, the French Revolution was the first triumphant political event with sufficient echos of change that it is yet to be achieved. The historian Paul Hazard paints a portrait of contrast:

---

[10] Cf., among all (our own library is already almost inexhaustible), Kant (1784), Todorov (2006), Plard (1986), Foucault (1993), pp. 61 et sq., *Qu'est-ce que les Lumières*, special issue (10) de "Dix-Huitième Siècle" , Paris, Garnier (1978), Cassirer (1966), Hazard (1961, 1979), Châtelet (1972), Chaunu (1982), Chouillet (1974), Didier (1987), Droixhe and Gossiaux (1985), Fabre (1963), Goyard-Fabre (1972), Gusdorf (1976), Jam (1992), *Lumières et Révolution*, special issue (6) of "Dix-Huitième Siècle", Paris, Garnier (1974), Mousnier and Labrousse (1985), Sgard et al. (1985), Starobinski (1987, 1989), Mortier (1982), Ehrhard (1970), Mauzy (1965), De Baecque and Mélonio (2005), Lichtenberger (1895), de Magalhães-Vilhena (1980), Portalis (1820), Rudé (1972), Trahard (1931, 1933), Willard (1963), del Carmen Rovira (1958), Mate and Niewöhner (1989), Herr (1960), Vovelle (1997), Blom (2004), Badinter (1999, 2002), Mornet (1989), Becker (1959), (1966).

[11] *Apud* http://www.prometheusonline.de/heureka/philosophie/klassiker/kant/aufklaerung.htm. … A possible translation, would be "Clarification" [Aufklärung] it means the exit of the men from His minority, from which is guilty of himself. The minority is the incapacity to make use of his understanding without a direction from another individual. The man is the own guilty of that minority if his cause is not in absence of understanding, but in the absence of decision and courage of serving himself without the direction of another. *Sapere aude!* It has the boldness of making use of his own understanding—this is the motto of Clarification [Aufklärung]. *Apud* http://serpensar.vilabol.uol.com.br/esclarecimento.htm.

[12] Naturally, and since the very beginning, with the pluralism that they bear: whether while epoch of free and disagreed thinkers amongst them a lot of times, whether has an epoch of synthesis, in which aspirations and legacies of several previous times converged. But always in the same line of emancipation. Cf., in this sense, Todorov (2006), pp. 9–10. Blending the "deep complexity of the cultural phenomenon of Illuminism", v.g., Baptista Pereira (1990), pp. 3 et sq.; cf. some aspects more historical of the Enlightenment in Portugal in de Oliveira Ramos (1988).

> Quel contraste! Quel brusque passage! La hiérarchie, la discipline, l'ordre que l'autorité se charge d'assurer, les dogmes qui règlent fermement la vie: voilà ce qu'aiment les hommes du dix-septième siécle. Les contraintes, l'autorité, les dogmes, voilà ce que détestent les hommes du dix-huitième siècle, leurs successeurs immédiats. Les premiers sont chrétiens, les autres antichrétiens; les premiers croient au droti divin, et les autres au droit naturel; les premiers vivent à l'aise dans une société qui se divise en classes inégales, les seconds ne rêvent qu'égalité."[13]

Jean Starobinski explains in depth what happened in the French Revolution and the mixture of the lights of reason with sinister and dark impulses.[14] Maybe a similar analysis would be useful to understand how the dreamed-of Republic has not yet been fully achieved to the present day. The text isn't very long, and it would be worth reading it all. Let's say with this synthesis, even though very incomplete, of the misfortune of the revolution: "By desiring to establish a kingdom of virtue, the revolutionary reason inevitably becomes suspicion's kingdom, and soon that of horror."[15]

But, if the achievements are imperfect, we should not think that it would be better not to dare. And it is by mistakes that we learn, as it is because of the dream that we keep on going.[16]

The Republic today is a lot more than the simple fact that the Head of the State (or the State's vertex, though merely a symbol) has to be elected and is temporarily in that position. On the contrary, monarchy does not change: the King is king lifelong and the office is hereditary.[17] Some old monarchies had an elective process, such as the Visigoth one. But that was long ago. A democratic mentality that does not give in to sentimentalist and traditionalist arguments without doubt chooses the first solution, the Republic. This happened, for example, in the referendum accomplished in Brazil (even though with all the criticisms that can be rightfully made to the referendums, which from the start was demagogy on the loose).[18] In spite of how very democratic a monarchy can be, it has always an anti-democratic vice of basis (and irremediable within its logic): that of the nation's supreme magistrate who is non-elected nor removable at the end of a relatively short amount of time.

Therefore, what is more the order of the day with republican thought, which once solved this question socially (without despising, naturally, the beliefs and monarchical activities of some, sometimes with a lot of activism, imagination,

---

13 Hazard (1961), p. VII.

14 Starobinski (1988).

15 Idem, Ibide, p. 48.

16 Sebastião da Gama, *Pelo Sonho é que Vamos, apud* http://belostextos.aaldeia.net/sonho-vamos.

17 Ribeiro (2008), pp. 24 et sq.

18 Cf., from the very beginning, Shaw (1944), p. 30: "But these assemblies of agitators must not be legislators. Such plausible pseudo-democratic devices as the Initiative and Referendum, which offer Mr. And Mrs. Everyman a direct immediate power to bind and lose, must be ruled out, because even when they know exactly what they want they do not know to get it, just as they may want a motor car, but cannot make the blue print which the engineer must have before he can construct one of them. Legislation must be by the 'quality', not by the mob." About the future of the representative democracy, v. the lucid observations of de Almeida Santos (2008), pp. 52 et sq.

intelligence and rhetorical cleverness, but always elitists and minorities—and, in our modest opinion, without reason), is precisely the problem of values and virtues related to the republican hope. When we speak about the Republic, it is the hope and not the routine that we are talking about.

3.7 Freedom

Paul Valéry clearly exaggerates when he puts the freedom question as follows:

> Liberté: cést un de ces détestables mots qui ont plus de valeur que de sens; qui chantent plus qu'ils parlent; qui demandent plus qu'ils ne répondent; de ces mots qui ont fait tous les métiers, et desquels la mémoire est barbouillée de Théologie, de Métaphysique, de Morale et de Politique; mots très bons pour la controverse, la dialectique, Íéloquence; aussi propres aux analyses illusoires et aux subtilités infinies quáux fins de phrase qui déchaînent le tonnerre.[19]

However, it is true that freedom has had many meanings and has been used for too many and sometimes clashing ideals… or less than ideal.[20]

In speaking of the value of republican liberty, we are not talking of course of pseudo-freedoms that are so exiguous in holders, or by absence of title are in fact nothing more than privileges or perks.

When we talk about freedom in a republican sense, we include rights and freedoms. And we are obviously talking about the *liberty of the moderns*, understood in the context of participatory democracy and even deliberative democracy,[21] where the old citizenship (the core of freedom of the ancients) is present, anew, without losing the force of *liberty of the moderns*, mainly garantistic principle: and this has also been deepened today.

Indeed, the neo-republicanism and deliberative democracy often go hand in hand. As can be deduced from this synthesis of Ricardo Pinto Leite, considering neorepublicanism as the normative theory of democracy, the more we reinforce our idea of republican democracy *tout court* as ethics, values, and virtues:

> The Neo-Republicanism is, then, a normative theory of democracy. There are several neo-republican approaches, some more liberal and others more communitarian in nature. It is possible, however, to identify at least three major common concerns, among others:
>
> (a) The civic virtue (*virtú*/civic virtue), designating involvement in the community, the preference for public interest, the search for common good as opposed to corruption (the incapability for the free life, the emergence of private interests, the "factions");

---

[19] Valéry (1945), *apud* Huisman and Salem (1982), p. 2.

[20] Petit (2001).

[21] Santiago Nino (1996), Dryzek (2000), Elster (1998), Macedo (1999), Gutman and Thompson (1996). And Ferreira da Cunha (2008), p. 159 et sq.

(b) The political participation that involves an extended process of discussion and deliberation where all can participate in independent and equal conditions (deliberative democracy) in which the argumentation in itself appeals to dialogical reason (*audi alteram partem*) and where conversational compromise gains a decisive importance;

(c) A certain model of citizenship and patriotism built around a civic conversation, the participation in the 'polis' with an emphasis in duty and responsibility.[22]

And the author goes on in a distinctive dialog with the liberal model:

This model, mainly in its deliberative position, intends to be an alternative to other theories of democracy, especially in a liberal perspective which is based in the aggregation of interest groups and in politic negotiation. The liberal model, centred in individualism, in individual rights and in the democracy of parties, would not have avoided the contemporary democratic crisis: corruption, citizens' withdrawal from political life, civic apathy, deficit in the legitimacy of political decisions.[23]

But let us try a more philosophical framing of the issue. When we speak of human freedom, it is supposed that we have already solved some problems, not unimportant, such as the degree of freedom of action of individuals and their degree of constraint, endogenous or exogenous, genetic, constitutional, on the one hand, social on the other. And although much free will and responsibility has made the person omnipotent, this may also be a powerful alibi to many penalties and charges. The truth (a heavy word ...) is that responsibility cannot easily be conceived without the idea that at least one other route could be traced by whom you invited to follow you. Never forgetting José Régio's poem:

"Come this way" - tell me with some candy eye
Stretching my arms, and insurance
what good would that I hear
When I say, "come here!"
I look at them with eyes weary,
(There is, in my eyes, tiredness and ironies)
And cross my arms,
And never go by there ... (...).[24]

And this is the secret of a free person: knowing how to say 'No'. And you can always say "No", as in the poem of Manuel Alegre, whose final stanza is also a hope, no longer just personal (Régio, on the other hand, was criticized for his non interventionist attitude, but not Alegre, who even suffered exile and after that, in democratic times, ran for President of the Republic) but political:

---

[22] Leite Pinto (2006), *apud* http://www.enelsyn.gr/papers/w7/Paper%20by%20Prof.%20Ricardo%20Leite%20Pinto.pdf.

[23] Ibidem.

[24] *Apud* http://www.releituras.com/jregio%5Fcantico.asp.

Even in the saddest night
in time of servitude
there's always someone who resists
there's always someone who says no.[25]

You may wonder about this approach to the value and nature of freedom, but the fact is that poets are those who best understand the values, and the most clear and deep expressions of those may be found in their poems, not in the dull and sad prose of boring academics. Certainly because poetry is a privileged way of communicating the most important things and expressing them. And values are some of the more important "things."

The question of free will leads us to inner freedom in comparison with the physical one. Both are accurate. You know there are the cases of a Pyrrhic victory or the sweet lemon syndrome: for example, the prisoner who boasts of his "freedom" in jail. Let us not blame the prisoner. What a great thing for him and for everyone to feel free. He is free, but inwardly. With this kind of freedom, societies do not live. This freedom is a witness (the martyrs are witnesses) and is an accusation. However, this freedom to be fully realized needs to be transposed to the streets, to cities, and to the political order.

On the other hand, freedom can reign, at least formally, in the political order (in societies where theoretically, that is to say, constitutionally, the rule of law reigns) and yet people do not feel they are free. The reasons for this can be varied.

Constitutional values, by definition, are cooperative and complementary: Freedom can be concerned if there is a lack of equality, or justice, or fraternity. We know that in a simple *laissez faire* freedom, without economic, social, and cultural aspects of basic equality is only freedom for some. This results in the ridiculous saying: "anyone has freedom of staying in a luxury hotel." Of course, but how many can afford it?

It may happen that freedom is too formal, just superstructural, and under the general freedom (electoral, media, etc.) the silent oppression of dictatorships germinates: micro-corporate, bureaucratic, local, etc.

Freedom needs to be cultivated, nurtured, and defended. Freedom is citizenship-based: for that, we need a solid background from childhood, or a powerful spirit that can overcome this lack of genius. And there is no such thing for many… Freedom is a learning process which begins in the family. And as today, so many confuse freedom with laxity, with parental absenteeism, with lack of education and also deficient firmness in education. Society forgets the need for participation, joint decision-making and dialog, composition, transactions, and compromise, but also "veto," in cases of dignity and questions of honor.

There is no freedom if there is no consciousness of freedom. And also where there is no permanent consciousness inevitably there are those who hate freedom, and those who will be indifferent either to freedom or to oppression. Especially if they just swim in a sea of happiness, alienated from what other people suffer.

---

[25] *Apud* http://users.isr.ist.utl.pt/~cfb/VdS/v008.txt.

And as a result, not only is an acute vigilance needed against total subversion of the democratic order (which may also exist: look up the sad but eloquent examples of the Weimar Republic, Salvador Allende's Chile in 1973, and many others, not far from us in time… just see what is going on in Hungary), but a patient pedagogy and diurnal tenacity.

First, by example, but also by the diffusion of ideas and debate. And it needs a lot of civic pedagogy, Republican pedagogy. Freedom, like health, often only can be appreciated when you lose it. Perhaps this would give reason to think of "suspending democracy" for a while, as some politicians already dare to say. A break in democracy would really be a huge boost to democratic and republican vocations. But of course we are not being serious: A suspension of democracy is always very bad. Some ingenuous observers and even learned people thought it would be a good idea in the past, but they regretted it deeply. A dictatorship (a suspension of democracy is always a dictatorship) is like a war: we know when it begins but we never know when it will end. All power wants to endure, and a dictatorship has more ways of enduring against the will of the People.

But without the shadow of ironies the issue of freedom cannot be taken as settled and resolved. At the frontiers of freedom, normal boundaries are always threatened from without and from within, and furthermore freedom always finds new expressions, and new challenges to be overcome.

Among the first rights of freedom were the freedom of religion and freedom of expression. Unfortunately, we must admit that neither of them are yet resolved. These two examples still have numerous problems: not only are there many countries where neither one is guaranteed, where people are persecuted, imprisoned and killed for defending them (or just because they express themselves), but also the set of interpretations and practices can subvert these major freedoms, even in countries that seem to enshrine them in their constitutions.

The proselytizing sects, the old privileges, prejudices of all stripes and from all walks entangle religious freedom to the point that there are many people in democratic countries who fear to express their ideas in this regard—whether belief, disbelief, or agnosticism. It depends on the small society where one moves. In some cases, we have to be one thing; in others, it is a sacrilege not to be another. In the work world there is sometimes a terrible fear of discrimination and, ultimately, one may lose his or her job because of hidden but real religious prejudices. This was for example the case in Greece, where some proselytizing religious officers harassed military personnel.[26]

Freedom of speech, leaving aside the difficulty of access to the media by ordinary mortals, is no guarantee of any real exercise of that freedom. And many circumstances can lead to silence. Even for a journalist through not only political and economic pressures, among others, may be forced into silence. The legal

[26] Guerreiro (2005).

system, conveniently manipulated by those who have money to hire perspicacious and persistent lawyers, can make the life of a free voice little less than hell.

With the slowness of assistance from the courts in virtually every country, a writer or a journalist whose nose, or more plausibly whose prose, displeases, can be soon silenced with processes. The poor and scarified people may win a claim, but actually, they are losing. Losing health, patience, and time, having too much trouble, and at having to pay the respective attorneys' fees, if they are not representing themselves in court, which never seems psychologically advisable.

In short, there are new freedoms not yet dreamed of that await our intuition and our creativity. And there are old freedoms which are hard to preserve and to prevent unfairness under fallacious pretexts. Too many people with a grain of power in their hands do not care about anything but more and more power, and the alibis used to make other people's life a hell are, of course, technocratic jargon: modernity, efficiency, changing times, etc. The good intentions of some are well-meaning, but for many the best alibi that our situation gives is to revanchist yesterday, just waiting for the moment to establish new prejudices, new rigid and illegitimate hierarchies, new retrograde policies.

Among the classic freedoms is the sacrosanct principle of the separation of powers, which no efficient complex system can justify ignoring. And to enforce it should be even deepened in a balanced and appropriate dissemination, even in the lower levels of the state. Where there is power and there is no separation of powers, free power is a wild beast: It will tend to increase its power and abuse. In a little-known text (originally in English), the always lucid Montesquieu says:

> The love of power is natural. It is insatiable, almost constantly whetted, never cloyed by possession.[27]

The tendency to want more power (and abuse it) is inevitable. So if we do not abuse but balance the powers (and that is a foundation of the Republic), the solution is to give rights to individuals, naturally, and special rights to citizens, special rights to employees, of course. But what are the rights that can be countered, equally, with enormous powers? They are other powers. So, power must be separated so that, by the celebrated mechanism of checks and balances, power confronts power. This is a lesson of Montesquieu, which should never fail to be present in the mind, and especially the heart, of today's politicians, because everyone benefits, even them. Luck is so capricious that to have absolute power today is a safe guarantee that tomorrow the dictator will not have a quiet retirement. Now this is more and more real because the tyrant may be assassinated (that is a very old risk, and many decided to take it). But things have changed a little bit: he may also be judged and put behind bars by a democratic and objective impartial court of justice, national or international, in his/her country or in a third State. The case of Pinochet is a very

[27] Montesquieu, *Spicilège*, n.º 525.

interesting example. The International Criminal Court is the first step to preventing those undemocratic situations. The next would be the International Constitutional Court.[28]

European Constitutions are full of freedoms (and rights and guarantees), at least in a traditional way. We believe that the future is imposing new demands, and new rights must be recognized. But we would be happy if the freedoms, rights, and political and social guarantees still present in the Constitutional texts of European countries, along with those in the European treaties, that are the European material Constitution, would be taken seriously,[29] which is less and less the case—especially for the social and propriety rights of common people.

But things may get better, and sometimes to make it better is the only way to survive. Take, for example, concerns on environmental and ecological matters. Just a few decades ago they were a marginal concern for political debate, very little assimilated by classical political forces. Today, there are ecological parties with some importance, and this is a front page concern. There is also an increasingly widespread awareness of this priority and vital global environmental rights.

Similarly, biological and gender questions, as well as IT and communication are profiled as main themes in the debate on rights for the future. This is not, however, the place to develop these issues either in balance or in prospective.

The problem of freedom has not been a special constitutional issue, nor in many cases, even a legal question. But problems arise from the application of value: by experience, administration, bureaucracy, de facto powers, and also other powers such as economic ones. Nowadays, an employer holds his or her employee almost in an *ius vitae ac necis*: because unemployment is now the general alternative to wage labor, and a matter of life or death, as seen in suicides among unemployed workers. Recently we have witnessed suicides of unemployed people evicted from their homes in Spain. We must admit that some old radicals were right: There is sometimes the freedom to starve. That is not freedom at all. When moderates have to give reason to some other positions, something is very "is rotten in the state of Denmark" (*Hamlet*, I, 4).

Another face of the debate is the criticism of monarchists against Republic. It is a rather minor question, but still Republics have to face it. Some monarchists say that in republican regimes there is no freedom, because many of them were established by a coup and never ratified by a popular referendum.

Although many support points can be put to referendums, exceptionally we would admit a referendum to end disputes definitely: if the monarchists solemnly undertook not to continue in their litany for, say, a hundred years at least … We are sure that such a consultation would be won overwhelmingly by the Republic, as happened in Brazilian referendum of 1993.

In fact, the referendum of the Republic has been common. In Portugal, where monarchists have recently been a small but very active minority, in every election

[28] Ben Achour (2014), Ferreira da Cunha (2014).

[29] Dworkin (1977).

the sympathetic monarchical party (it was the first ecologic party in the country) ran alone, it never managed to elect a single MP. In some countries, at least, monarchism seems to be more of a family tradition or, in the best case a solipsistic intellectual option of some "happy few." It has its charms, of course, and some people may be seduced by the fairy tale narrative.

Freedom, however, is far above the issues of regime. And against the wise skeptic Paul Valéry, we prefer the more confident and even enthusiastic Paul Eluard and his long poem on freedom, which ends:

> Et par le pouvoir d'un mot□
> Je recommence ma vie□
> Je suis né pour te connaître□
> Pour te nommer
> Liberté.[30]

3.8 Equality

Almost at the beginning of his small but precious book Rousseau wrote; *Du contrat social*: "L'homme est né libre, et partout il est dans les fers."[31]

But it is more than that: People (each person) are free and equal according to the Declaration of the Rights of Man and of the Citizen of 1789, one of the finest and wisest Republican primary texts. In its first article it proclaims, not only for XVIIIth century France, but for everyone and all time, the awareness that this corresponds to the discovery of a universal political truth:

> Article premier - Les hommes naissent et demeurent libres et égaux en droits. Les distinctions sociales ne peuvent être fondées que sur l'utilité commune.[32]

It is not only the natural and intrinsic right of human freedom, but also equality. And this could still mean something symmetrical to that noted for freedom by the citizen of Geneva. Equality is not a prisoner, but is absent, mystified, deformed, even reviled.

The first major error affecting equality, and this was a flank offered to their detractors, is due to collectivism and its confusion with egalitarianism (though there are authors that exchange the words and the meanings…). In any case, equality is not the apparently same uniform, nor the bed of Procrustes that shrinks the highs

[30] Eluard (1942).

[31] Rousseau (1762), I, 1.

[32] *Apud* http://www.textes.justice.gouv.fr/index.php?rubrique=10086&ssrubrique=10087&article=10116.

and distends the lows. Being equal is not to be a photocopy of others. Equality, in addition to its bourgeois version of equality before the law (short, but the basic, the elementary version: it all starts there), does not justify "exceptions," such as favoritism and corruption; it is more, much more than that. It is now, in a word, the welfare state in its classic European version: the "European social model," that is in danger at least in the countries under speculative attack. This model can go much further of course, first with the advancement of Fraternity. But for now it has to consolidate itself, and proves to its terrible enemies that it is not only suitable, but sustainable. One of the most intelligent and eloquent defenses of the welfare state comes from the pen of the great Brazilian constitutionalist Paulo Bonavides. Always along the lines of the co-implication of values, the welfare state is a concrete way of making the principles of liberty, equality, and fraternity real.[33] Of course not at their maximum, but in a certain possible concretisation. We would like to quote this important author, because of the clarity of his ideas and the rousing style of his speech. He explains the difference among the diverse kinds of social states very well and it is obvious which one he prefers, and we prefer—a social and democratic state, with rule of law, in the true sense of the terms:

> We distinguish in our study two main modalities of the welfare state: the social state of Marxism, where dirigism is imposed from top to bottom, with the abolition of capitalist infrastructure and the consequent social ownership of the means of production (...), and the state of social democracy, which admits the same idea of dirigism, with the only difference that here it is a consented dirigism, from bottom to top, which keeps the foundations of capitalism intact.[34]

There were other welfare or social states: even right wing ones, such as the fascist state, or the "New State"—*Estado Novo*—in Brazil and Portugal, which in their last phase, replaced their advertised expression "corporative state" with "social state".

But now, more than ever, the social state is the object of a very large ideological consensus, although the media, largely tuned with neoliberal powers, does not transmit that reality: a social state with rule of law is what many different parties and ideologies want: because it opens up all the windows of democratic socialism, the deepening of social democracies, the more demanding and consequential social democratic tendencies and of social-liberalism, and Christian democrats committed to the word of Gospel, even of Communist renovators who accept the rules of democracy and the market, traditionalists with social sensibility, etc., But the base is in the common denominator, the welfare state. That is a principle in everything upheld by republicanism. It is the same as Rousseau said, adding freedom and equality symptomatically because they are linked, and it is a profound fallacy, today only sustainable by naivety or bad faith, arguing for freedom against equality, as do the neoliberals, or for equality against freedom, as they would if they were sincere collectivists:

---

[33] Bonavides (2004), p. 36.

[34] Ibidem, p. 25.

> J'ai déjà dit ce que c'est que la liberté civile: à l'égard de l'égalité, il ne faut pas entendre par ce mot que les degrés de puissance et de richesse soient absolument les mêmes; mais que, quant à la puissance, elle soit au-dessus de toute violence, et ne s'exerce jamais qu'en vertu du rang et des lois; et, quant à la richesse, que nul citoyen ne soit assez opulent pour en pouvoir acheter un, autre, et nul assez pauvre pour être contraint de se vendre: ce qui suppose, du côté des grands, modération de biens et de crédit, et, du côté des petits, modération d'avarice et de convoitise.[35]

Equality is an end and also a means. Shining at the end of the tunnel it still has hazy outlines for us. Anyway, we must consent here that one way of moving toward equality is in the deepening of Social Justice. This is discussed in a separate chapter, after speaking about justice in general.

We cannot forget that one means of achieving equality and political measures (which may have, and largely assume legal form) is Law. And there is a legal principle of equality (not just a value), as, there is a legal principle of justice and rights of Freedom (Freedoms). To a very large measure the problems about law start with the interpretation, which is never easy because there are never simple cases, and even an apparently obvious bill can in many cases be distorted by the concepts and prejudices of the interpreter. Nor can one say that there is neutrality in this regard, although the great jurists, ethically need to be aware of their prejudices in order to cope well with them. Everything may be controversial, and always may be subject to different doctrine.[36]

But one thing is certain and elementary: one cannot, with tricks and interpretive skills, offend the spirit of the constitution and the general spirit of modern societies, which is one of equal treatment.

The way to the very recognition of the idea "equality" is painful. Despite the open nature and culture of its organizers, the "great ideas of Western civilization," linked to the "great books," coordinated by Mortimer Adler, encompassed approximately 102 concepts for years. "Equality" was the last to be considered, and only later integrated in the list.[37]

3.9 Justice

'Justice' is a very polysemic word. There are three senses of Justice that may interest us now above all.

The first one, which is yet to be put in the shadow, because the political and juridical value "Justice" does not reach such high levels, is the idea of Justice as moral authority, or moral virtue and value, both if we want. It hovers in the highest

---

[35] Rousseau (1762) II, 11.

[36] de Albuquerque (1993), Bandeira de Mello (2008). This last author arrived to some important conclusions on the constitutional principle of isonomy, not far from equality.

[37] Adler (2000), p. XI.

of human things, if they are human. Aristotle says (quoting Euripides[38]), and Aquinas does not fail to mention: "The most resplendent virtues seems to be Justice, nor the evening star nor the morning star are so admirable."[39]

This is the result of a moral or general Justice which, as Aristotle points out quoting the poet Theognis of Megara,[40] "contains all the virtues" or "embraces all the virtues".[41]

But such a high idea of Justice may be excessive to current life and inadequate to politics. Sometimes it is not always the most virtuous in the overall plan which is best suited to specifically political virtue. The classic example of this separation between private vices and public virtues is *The Fable of the Bees.*[42] But still worthy of consideration are the latest comments from Ortega y Gassett on Mirabeau.[43] Mirabeau was not personally too virtuous, on the contrary. But could his political (not personal) moderation, ductility and political genius not have saved France of Terror, in fact a kind of an excess of virtue? Worth reading Ortega... which is at least one alternative and very seductive historical hypothesis. *Si non è vero...* Montesquieu had also maturely understood the difference between moral virtue and political virtue:

> Je n'ai point dit ceci pour diminuer rien de la distance infinie qu'il y a entre les vices et les vertus: à Dieu ne plaise! J'ai seulement voulu faire comprendre que tous les vices politiques ne sont pas des vices moraux, et que tous les vices moraux ne sont pas des vices politiques; et c'est ce que ne doivent point ignorer ceux qui font des lois qui choquent l'esprit général.[44]

There is also a second important sense of Justice: particular Justice, specifically legal, which results in a compression resulting from an epistemic limitation issuing from that first sense, in which Justice is a virtue. That virtue, in this second sense, descends to earth and humanizes itself. It is a matter of Law. The field of law is large, but law is always limited by some guidelines. Just, in this sense, it is not Job, the highest medieval Biblical example of Justice who is taken as a model, but the much less admirable Roman honest citizen, the *bonus paterfamilias*, who pays his bills, exactly as he should: he is not even a gentleman who gives more than receives ... To be just, to practice Justice in this sense is not to be a saint, a hero, a gentleman. Just fair in paying what is due. In this case, the specific legal rigor defines Justice by the formula of Justinian's Digest, which hosts the sentence engraved in Gold letters in the juridical memory by Ulpianus: "constans et perpetuates voluntas suum cuique tribuendi".

Justice is, consequently, a constant and perpetual will to give each one what is his or hers. Of course, the problem is to know what is each one's due, as is well observed by Norberto Bobbio, among others. However, the answer is usually this:

---

38 Euripides, fr. of *Melanippe* (Nauck, fr. 486).

39 Aristotles, *Nicomachean Ehics*, V, 1129 a.

40 Theognis, 147: εν δε δικαιοσυνη συλληβδην πασ απετη στι.

41 Identical to Phocylides, 17.

42 Mandeville (1988).

43 Ortega y Gasset (1982).

44 Montesquieu (1748) XIX, 11.

the *suum* of each person is what each one has the right to hold by force of a legal title. But here again the problem ensues. What then are legal titles? Legal titles may be defined easily. The problem comes next. They are accepted forms (by a legal order) to create, modify, maintain or terminate legal relationships or legal situations. Hence, we can give as examples the law, custom, contract, testament, the original acquisition (immediately by hunting and fishing), etc. To this strict list (actually a little bigger), some authors, not so rigorist, discovered an obstacle: The problem of Social Justice. But they also found a way out of the impasse: the recognition of human dignity and that is also a juridical title.

Let us comment on it a little bit more. A person does not have only what comes in a contract, will, etc.; that is his or her *suum*. And what would happen if someone had nothing or too little (the case of indigence, even severe poverty) from these sources? Should society and the State let him or her starve? As Agostinho da Silva put it: cries and laughs (poverty and wealth) are separated by tall hedges. So, it is a terrible fate for the police and for the judge if they are supposed to give the rich their property and punish the poor who disturb that property. Their role must be better than that.

What happened was that, given the glaring inequality, some jurists began to think that a minimum standard of living at least should be guaranteed to each and every one regardless of any other consideration. And which legal title would justify a guaranteed minimum income, a social insertion income, or something else? No more nor less than the very condition of being a Person. Being a Person is the highest legal title, and one that gives the right to the provision of social survival, by the law, freedoms and guarantees of more political bent, etc.

Obviously, those who wanted a pure law, strictly isolated and protected, forevermore apart from considerations of "politics" and "ideology," a purely "legal" law could not be satisfied with this form of desecration of legal titles, those that so accurately separated what was legal and what was not. But things are as they are: this consideration of mankind in legal titles caused numerous problems for supporters of abstract theories. But even if it was not a perfect theoretical construction, the fact is that it works. And the trees must be judged by their fruits.[45]

From this or some other way, then arises the third sense of Justice. And this is very important in constitutional terms. It is Social Justice.[46]

3.10 Justice, Social Justice and Republic

Justice as an approach to value is a more evaluative account of the requirements of fairness in the application of law to concrete situations. Dealing not only with a strict conception of the *cuique suum* precept, but also calling for the ideals of social

---

[45] Lc., VI, 43-44.

[46] About Welfare state and social justice, v.g., Ferreira da Cunha (2005), pp. 87 et sq., Ferreira da Cunha (2003, 2012), Ackerman (1993), Boudon (1995), Tale (1995), pp. 245–291; Guérard Latour (2003), Craveiro da Silva (1994).

justice for all, especially with attention to the poor and marginalized. Justice must always integrate equity (although it is sometimes separated). But fairness must not be used to subvert the value of equality. They are different things, at different levels. Equality requires, for example, the universality of a National Health Service equity (in our Portuguese case already established—thankfully, although in great danger now) requires that they pay attention to the extent of actual features, such as mitigating and aggravating circumstances.

Some concrete experiences of the Republic led some authors, particularly some of the most profound fans of social transformation to criticize the Republic as it would be contrary to Social Justice, or at least very shy in this matter. One could say, extending an argument of Harold Nicolson, that young republics, as young people, must be shy and gain from it.[47] But it is not a good argument, because the sum of endurance among all republics give the Republic, at least in some countries, a considerable age.

One has to always distinguish what is achieved in real and in promised ideals. Republics have not always really done what they wanted. But let us not blame the ideals by the concrete error or difficulties. It is the human syndrome of the "arrow of Nimrod."[48] But we should counteract this prejudice. Levy-Bruhl, analyses this current topic quite well. Indeed, people have already forgotten what it was like before the Republic:

> The vices of the old monarchy, the ignominy of the imperial regime, are only known from books. The weaknesses and difficulties of the current regime, we see them and feel them. They lie to the eyes, shoulders overwhelm us with all their weight. A bad thing now looks ever more unbearable than a greater evil that we had no experience of. Hence the harsh judgments that even good Republicans cast upon our current institutions.[49]

He continues, marking the distinctions between the real and ideal. But he never considers the ideal just as an unattainable chimera:

> That said, we confess that our system is still far from the ideal Republic. Often political hypocrisy serves to mask social inequity. Often the beautiful name of republican institutions simply covers the means to satisfy appetites of affluence and ignoble selfishness. But is the republican ideal therefore, attained, diminished, or soiled?
>
> No way, just as the religious ideal of the Christian is not compromised if the indignity of such and such a servant operates for their benefit.[50]

Specifically talking about social issues, the author is very clear in rejecting some hesitation in this area:

> Presenting yourself as Republican and the same time opposing, openly or covertly, the reforms that social justice demands, is a flagrant contradiction or a ignoble lie.[51]

---

[47] Nicolson (1987), pp. 305 et sq.

[48] Serra (2002), pp. 41 et sq.

[49] Levy-Bruhl (s.d.), p. 6.

[50] Idem, Ibidem.

[51] Ibidem, p. 7.

And the author even identifies the republican ideal with social justice, saying:

> The first requirement of the republican ideal, i.e., social justice, soon appears clearly. It orders to fight and if it is possible to remove everything in institutions that promotes, sustains, perpetuates oppression and exploitation of a part of citizens of another one.[52]

The conclusion of this reasoning is not only legal but also political. The French writer is for the abolition of privileges, sometimes pretending to be acquired rights:

> The republican ideal, which requires Justice, therefore demands an end to abuses which necessarily engender the predominance of a class – the possessing class today, or more accurately the holders of money, the plutocracy. The privileges, which hide under the respectable appearance of acquired rights, should disappear.[53]

Of course not all acquired rights are privileges. Some are bastions of labor conquests, and the line that divides dignity from servitude.

Evidently the Republic should not be confused with any egalitarianism, collectivism, etc. Inequalities exist in the Republic. But not *inequality* as an invincible reality and as a principle of social life. For as Régis Debray says, it is a society in which conditions (naturally diverse) correspond to the merits of each and not to heredity. Besides, in harmony with the general outlook of John Rawls: basic equality, is inequality based on the social contribution of each.[54]

3.11 Fraternity

Fraternity, according to the Italian jurist Eligio Resta (but not only according to him), is the least accomplished value of the French Revolution (actually, he speaks of an "Enlightenment Revolution," which seems to be a good expression). In the summary of his work, on the theme chosen for its cover, it is stated:

> La fraternità è stata la grande promessa mancata della Rivoluzione illuminista. Affacciatasi allora, è rimasta, non a caso, la parente povera di quel progetto. Oggi ritorna con tutti i suoi paradossi, ma con la stessa forza, dinanzi alla 'vecchia storia' della guerra e di un nuovo, contrastante bisogno di cosmopolitismo. Impone così la riflessione su un diritto fraterno, capace di superare gli egoismi che si nascondono tra le piegje dei globalismi arroganti.[55]

More recently still, the diagnostic of Regis Debray is not essentially different. But it should be noted that the author points the finger at the liberal society:

---

52 Ibidem, p. 9.

53 Ibidem, p. 10.

54 Rawls (1971).

55 Resta (2002).

> La fraternité est le mal-aimé de la société libérale, traité avec condescendance par la haute *intelligentsia*, et superbement ignoré para nos autorités en place.[56]

But today, we know more peacefully that Liberty could also have been more and better established and would have been helped by more equality, but this also fell short, often precisely because of lack of freedom. Both have a deficit, although the most forgotten was Fraternity, which is the largest and most difficult of all: until now always in last place, or no place at all.

However, Fraternity (may we say: as occurs in the triad of the Trinity with the Holy Spirit?[57]) may have a subtle presence… as it seems so eloquently expressed in this "confession" of Supreme Court Justice Stephen Breyer:

> Le sujet exact de cette conférence concerne le principe de la fraternité au sein des Constitutions. On s'attend à dire qu'un tel principe n'existe pas dans la Constitution américaine - jusqu'à ce que l'on commence à penser sérieusement au sujet. Alors l'on se rend compte que le principe de la fraternité se manifeste au fond de la Constitution américaine. Certes on ne peut jeter aucun coup d'oeil sur le terrain du droit américain sans le trouver partout.[58]

But this subtle Fraternity is pedagogical: it turns out to be a signal for us to have the greatest care in its invocation and in projects about it. Even less subtle was communism (understood as the final and crowning stage of evolution of humanity) and Marx, wise and sensitive to the concept, protested that he would not describe it, he would not do the "menus for the taverns of the future."

But the subtle Fraternity, with the utmost care, needs to move to the forefront of concerns of future *polis*. And the Republic with new breath should make it a flag: if not the main one, a very important one. Because Fraternity, and it alone, is capable of overcoming and arbitrate even conflicts between Liberty and Equality, which dominated the debate in the last century (e.g.: 'liberalisms' vs. 'socialisms'). As stated by Ayres Britto, former President of the Brazilian Supreme Court of Justice:

> Not coincidentally, Fraternity is the point of the unity that can be reached by conciliation between the extremes of Liberty on one side, and on the other, Equality. It is the proof that also in the fields of Law and Politics virtue is always in the middle (*medius in virtus*). With the full understanding, however, that it is not possible to attain this unity without first going through the dualities.[59]

Fraternity, being a moral and political value, can actually manifest itself in law—almost "by paradox."

---

[56] Debray (2009), p. 96. Debray (2010).

[57] Despite the unorthodox image, you can not forget that there is a modern theology (with a feminist slant) that explicitly considers the Holy Spirit as "the principle of equal relations' but with a being classified as' sweet', which somehow in can think of Fraternity. Rocha (2008), pp. 19 et sq.

[58] *Réflexions relatives au principe de fraternité*: http://www.supremecourtus.gov/publicinfo/speeches/sp%5F06-20-03.html (issued at Ottawa Congress of the Association of Constitutional Courts of the French language, on June 20, 2003).

[59] Ayres de Brito (2006), p. 218.

More talk will not suffice in Fraternal Law, a designation that risks a pseudo-unanimous ambience, beneficent but without rigor. Fraternal law in its proper sense is a legal concretization of the value of Fraternity, and this is a value with a deeply humanistic tone. Because the suggestion already seems to be in the air, inspiring us from a more recent work of Ayres de Britto[60], at this moment we would venture that the new paradigm for Law would be a Humanist Fraternal Law. It may be a big concept in words: and for sure it is in substance … Let us not be concerned with marketing of scientific designations: Things must have the name of their nature, or the closest possible to a description of their meaning...

Anyway, the cold steel of the swords of law (which translated the maxim of Roman decadence *dura lex sed lex*), as the former lawyer and writer Teixeira de Pascoaes described as the excessive roughness of law, must first give place to the classic rule of Lesbos, mentioned by Aristotle, which conforms to any surface that it would measure.[61] But that is still justice in its dimension of fairness. Fraternity is so far above this dimension that we even have difficulty to exemplify it in the present state of the law, even averse to equity in so many ways. It is indeed significant that many of the examples given as being fraternity are actually cases of Equity or Equality. How far it is even from our ability to dream...

However, it is very easy to recognize from the outset that Fraternity applies today, in a special way, to the idea of brotherhood between persons across borders. Internationally there is now a great place for Fraternity. And the right to peace is a right of brotherhood. We cannot forget that the right to peace is, in the words of Paul Bonavides, "the supreme law of Humanity."[62]

Besides Peace, the defence of Human Rights, which has of course dimensions of natural Freedom (perhaps this is the most notorious for the blatant violations of Human Rights that continue to occur) and Equality (which sounds warning cries of famine and epidemics in less developed countries), is also a duty of the international Fraternity.

How far the European Union is today from the idea of Fraternity and even simple solidarity: many treat the Greeks as if they had a plague (it is the fear of financial contagion) in their present misfortune, compounded especially by international greed. And this distain for the Greeks may soon include others. If Europe does not give an example of true solidarity (not only through aid, but in lowering usurious interest: and debts, one way or another, should be forgiven, because nobody can, even in the worst misery—and specially in poverty—pay such interest) vain diplomatic or media declarations and policies will not attain European cohesion. We are going back decades in the building of a European soul, a real European cohesion… Following the present course of cuts and misery to the public and good opportunities only to those who are already very rich (the middle class is vanishing) not only there will be no cohesion at all but, on the contrary, Europe will crumble.

---

60 Ayres de Brito (2007).

61 Aristotle, *Nicomachean Ethics*, V, 14 (1137 b).

62 Bonavides (2008), p. 593.

Moreover, given the current circumstances, we believe that, sadly, the great project of a united Europe is seriously compromised at the level of the image and hope for the European project (and also, of course, constitutional culture[63]). Among peoples of the South, at least: many do not regard the European Union and its rules as anything good, and they miss the time when there was no Euro, but their national currencies. It does not matter for now and for our current perspective if economically and financially they are right or wrong. Perceptions are what they are, and have the consequences that they have, not considering their justification and truth. That is the sad sociological reality, which should make all European enthusiasts (like ourselves) take a serious examination of their conscience. Unfortunately, this European situation is not federalism. And the problems arise from the exacerbation of some nationalism. In many cases, the ones that complain the loudest are those who pay the highest percentage to Europe. That is, in many countries this lack of Fraternity, and even the absence of the most basic solidarity, can endanger their Freedom, and obviously inequalities are rising inside countries and among them. So, the constitutional architecture of Europe may come to a moment of rupture. We hope, along with many others, that we are wrong.

Internally, it is evident that society should express solidarity with the needy, but this must begin with an attitude of civic spirit and citizenship, of non-prejudice, non-discrimination, and without exaggeration of personal self-concept. Fraternity is not charity: It is a higher form of solidarity and social justice. By the way: in these times of trouble, "a little charity," from some people who like to appease their conscience by giving away something they don't need at all (and others with just good will) tend to try to replace true solidarity. Unfortunately there is not enough awareness of the enormous difference between charity, solidarity, and, of course, Fraternity. And we mean charity as a slushy old-fashioned and full of prejudice charity: not charity as "love," of course. Even Fraternity is not yet Love. But these days who really loves those in need and the consequences of that? Words may be nice, but acts are much more important. And—in moral terms—we must consider the psychological disposition with which acts are made and the personal circumstances of the action (the gift, for example). The small widow's mite would be always much more positive and praiseworthy in moral terms than the large Pharisaic grant.[64]

Seen in this Light, after a colorful history the Republic is more seasoned and conscious nowadays, and has some advantages over other constructions. The idea that someone makes himself to be inherently superior to others for having "blue blood" is very dangerous for society and also for the one who thinks it, undoubtedly giving place to severe social conflicts and perhaps some personal frustrations (beginning with those "nobles" who are never given enough "consideration" in a democratic society: and must suffer continuous "outrages" to their high rank…). Because, fortunately, our European societies, although some keep a decorative King, are essentially republican. Apart from the "happy few" families (and not all

---

[63] See Ferreira da Cunha (2012).

[64] Mr., XII, 41–44; Lc. XI, 1–4.

those members), only those mentalities which delight in social columns, are still interested in nobilities of blood. There is still a residue of underdevelopment manifest in certain levels of our societies, especially among those who aspire to be in those social columns because they think they have or they pretend to have that blue blood, or dream they night marry a Prince charming (maybe also a royal *sleeping beauty*?) and become noble through the 'magic' of social climbing. In fact, many poor people feed their dreams with that ghost of identification with kings and queens, princes and princesses ... and all the ranges of the complex noble hierarchy. It is the Cinderella complex. Some sell those dreams very well.

Fraternity is incompatible with a conception of genetic nobility, aristocracy (in fact oligarchy) of blood. For, regardless of birth, Fraternity is not only based on equality between all, which in itself could be just arithmetic, but an active equal communion as siblings... It is interesting to note that, virtue being the main principle of republics it is by the test of virtue that La Bruyère conveys nobility (whose principle—indeed since the Greeks, and even Aristotle—is honor[65]), in these incisive terms:

> Si la noblesse est vertu, elle se perd par tout ce qui n'est pas vertueux; et si elle n'est pas vertu, c'est peu de chose.[66]

But in return, Fraternity is not in any way contrary to the existence of elites. For elites, not oligarchies (so often confused) are a condition to the existence of the Republic. No Republic can survive without elites. Just be aware that there are differences: there is a persistent vice in considering as an elite just a group with power or money, which is very wrong: power itself has nothing to do with an elite if it is just *potestas*, not *auctoritas*. And money has really nothing to do with it. Nor of course does privileged birth.

But the Republic does not need just any elites: only democratic and demophilic ones. Brussels, the symbolic head of European Union, must have elites, not a bureaucracy, as do the different states in their governments and public administrations. A bureaucrat follows orders and a routine. Elite thinkers contribute in a democratic spirit to new and better solutions. The bureaucrat aims for his or her retirement, because, with the exception of some power maniacs, he or she does not like working. The member of an elite feels rewarded by the work he or she does. Because it is by his or her work that his or her mark on the world is made.

The elite in government depend on both the people's wisdom to vote well and choose the best, and the parties' wisdom to select the candidates well among party members and independent candidates appointed by the parties. It is not easy from both sides. Elites in public administration depends on governmental wisdom (and of administration itself to a certain extent, because government cannot decide and control everything and nominate all civil servants).

---

[65] Jaeger (1936, 1979), p. 28; Aristotle, *Nicomachean Ethics*, 1095 b, 26.

[66] La Bruyère (1688), XIV, 15.

Because of a certain disillusion with the people's choice and party appointments, we had that excellent satire "Yes, Minister" and "Yes, Prime Minister".[67] We have no doubt that the idea is inherent in this TV series. Sometimes the high civil servant, Sir Humphrey, is the only wise man, taking control of a demagogic and rather foolish Minister or Prime Minister. So, he is part the good elite. Nevertheless, some other times we see a clever and wise Minister or Prime Minister not letting themself be deceived for a rather conservative and frozen "Sir," and opening the way to progressive or at least just measures. And so, the Minister is part of a democratic elite. In this particular case, the balance between those two rationalities is interesting, and we see good dialectics in the halls of power.

As stated by the French philosopher and sociologist Levy-Bruhl, a lucid Republic theorist, for democracy (but with the same reason it could be for the Republic):

> Democracy is not (…) blind enough to believe you can dismiss an elite. But what distinguishes it from the previous regimes is that it doesn't want this elite imposed already made, or recruited exclusively or preferably among the members of a single social class. It must be confessed, moreover, that at this point we are also far from the ideal.[68]

Once again, there is not much to be invented, but many things wait for a real, practical application. And it depends a lot, again, on social values and individual virtues and identification with those values being put into practice.

The issue of republican elites as opposed to aristocracies and oligarchies of blood (a very different thing is the aristocracy of mind and actions, in fact identical to the republican elite) has been strongly emphasized in the opposition between the concepts of "grands seigneurs" and "grands hommes" in the classic Encyclopedia directed by Denis Diderot and D'Alembert, a powerful instrument of revolutionary mentalities that preceded the French Revolution. So begins the respective article, by the Knight of Jaucourt:

> Seigneur *grand*, Homme *grand*, (*Langue franç.*) ces deux expressions, *grand seigneur, & grand homme* n'indiquent point une même chose; il s'en faut de beaucoup; les *grands seigneurs* sont communs dans le monde, & les *grands hommes* très-rares; l'un est quelquefois le fardeau de l'état, l'autre en est toujours la ressource & l'appui. La naissance, les titres, & les charges font un *grand seigneur*; le rare mérite, le génie & les talens éminens font un *grand homme*. Un *grand seigneur* voit le prince, a des ancêtres, des dettes & des pensions; un *grand homme* sert sa patrie d'une maniere signalée, sans en chercher de récompense, sans même avoir aucun égard à la gloire qui peut lui en revenir. Le duc d'Epernon & le maréchal de Retz étoient de *grands seigneurs;* l'amiral de Coligny & la Noue étoient de *grands hommes*.

[67] Lynn and Jay (1984, 1986). There are also vídeos of the series.

[68] Levy-Bruhl (s.d.) p. 12.

Quand les Romains furent corrompus par les richesses des provinces conquises, on commença à voir naître de leur avilissement, l'époque du nom de *grand seigneur*, & le philosophe réserva le titre de *grand homme* à ces rares mortels qui aiment, qui servent & qui éclairent leur pays. Celui qui obtient une noble fin par de nobles moyens, qui disgracié rit dans l'exil & dans les fers, soit qu'il regne comme Antonin, ou qu'il meure comme Socrate, celui-là est un *grand homme* aux yeux des sages; mais les simplement *grands seigneurs* n'ont par-dessus les hommes ordinaires qu'un peu de vernis qui les couvre (...).[69]

The elites must not only exist, and see their existence supported, for what they are worth. In fact, it is like John Rawls's theory of inequality only by merit, on an equal basis.[70]

In short, among all republican values, the furthest away is still Fraternity. But there is now a clearer diagnosis of the reasons for that situation, and we begin to understand that you cannot wait for the consummation of Liberty to pass Equality or Justice, and for the realization of all these to finally work for Fraternity. We must work on all these values together, and it seems that the Fraternity is a kind of love for Equality and Freedom. As in some metaphors about the Holy Spirit... Fraternity, *cum grano salis*, could be called Freedom and Equality's *holy spirit.*

3.12 Value Topics: Citizenship, Pluralism, Secularism, Legal Certainty and Governance

There are still axiological topics that, in everyday language, are quite often treated as values sensu *proprio*. They lack the size, high level, and quality which real values have, and in each case, it is not difficult to put them under the auspices of one or more values. Citizenship and Pluralism, for example, are manifestations of Freedom, especially. Although, of course, there are also aspects of Equality they also touch. All values are related, as we know.

These topics do not need further development for our present case, although they are not self-evident. Let us enumerate the most important among them: They are citizenship and pluralism, cited above, and also laicity (*laicité*), the secular state (which manifests itself in a real equanimity and equal treatment of all faiths, indifferences, agnosticisms and atheisms), legal certainty (the zero degree of justice: we must know the law where we live), and governance. On this last one, Ulysses Guimarães, president of the Brazilian Constituent Assembly though the President of the Republic, and who was concerned about the issue said:

(...) The governance is social. Hunger, poverty, ignorance, unassisted disease are ungovernable.

[69] Chevalier de Jaucourt, "Grand Seigneur", *Encyclopédie*, org. Diderot/D'Alember, t. XIV. *Apud* http://fr.wikisource.org/wiki/Page:Diderot%5F-%5FEncyclopedie%5F1ere%5Fedition%5Ftome%5F14.djvu/895.

[70] Rawls (1971).

Social injustice is the denial and condemnation of government. (…) This Constitution, the Brazilian people allow me to proclaim it, will not be as beautiful unfinished statue, mutilated or desecrated. The people sent us here to do it, not to be afraid (…).[71]

Governments must govern, not to be concerned about the existence of checks and balances. These are normal in a Constitutional state. They do not exist to irritate ministers, but to protect citizens either from their voluntarism, or their apathy in office. When a person who rules, at any level, complains about the counter powers or the excess of legalism, or the restrictions on their work by the law courts, we may be certain that the person is with high probability an authoritarian mind. And we know where, with favorable winds, all these minds may lead a country, or a continent.

References

Ackerman, B. (1993). *Social justice in the liberal state.* Spanish trad and introduction by Carlos Rosenkrantz, *La Justicia Social en el Estado Liberal.* Madrid: Centro de Estudios Constitucionales.

Adler, M. (2000). *The great ideas from the great books of western civilization.* In M. Weismann (ed.), 2nd print. Chicago, La Salle: Open Court.

Ayres de Brito, C. (2006). *Teoria da Constituição.* Rio de Janeiro: Forense.

Ayres de Brito, C. (2007). *O Humanismo como Categoria Constitucional.* Belo Horizonte: Forum.

Badinter, E. (1999). *Les passions intellectuelles. Désir de gloire (1735–1751).* Paris: Fayard.

Badinter, E. (2002). *Les passions intellectuelles. Exigence de dignité (1751–1762).* Paris: Fayard.

Bandeira de Mello, C. A. (2008). *Conteúdo Jurídico do Princípio da Igualdade* (3rd ed.). São Paulo: Malheiros.

Baptista Pereira, M. (1990). *Modernidade e Secularização.* Coimbra: Almedina.

Becker, C. L. (1959). *The heavenly city of eighteenth-century philosophers* (12th ed.). New Haven: Yale University Press.

Becker, C. L. (1966). *The declaration of independence. A study in the history of political ideas*, 9th rep. New York: Alfred A. Knopf.

Ben Achour, Y. (2014). *Au Service du droit démocratique et du droit constitutionnel international. Une Cour constitucionnelle internationale.* "Revue du Droit Public et de la Science Politique en France et à l'estranger". Paris: LGDJ, n.º 2, pp. 419–443.

Blom, P. (2004). *Encyclopédie.* London: Fourth Estate/Harper Collins.

Bonavides, P. (2004). *Do Estado Liberal ao Estado Social* (7th ed.). São Paulo: Malheiros Editores.

Bonavides, P. (2008). *Curso de Direito Constitucional* (24th ed.). São Paulo: Malheiros.

Bonavides, P., & de Andrade, P. (1991). *História Constitucional do Brasil.* São Paulo: Paz e Terra.

Boudon, R. (1995). *Le Juste et le Vrai.* Paris: Fayard.

Cassirer, E. (1966). *La Philosophie des Lumières.* Paris: Fayard.

Châtelet, F. (Ed.). (1972). *Les Lumières.* Paris: Hachette.

Chaunu, P. (1982). *La Civilisation de l'Europe des Lumières.* Paris: Flammarion.

Chouillet, J. (1974). *L'esthetique des lumières.* Paris: P.U.F.

[71] *Apud* Bonavides and de Andrade (1991), p. 466. And also Ferreira da Cunha (2009b), pp. 158 et sq.

Craveiro da Silva, L. (1994). Marxismo, filosofia da libertação. *Ensaios de Filosofia e Cultura Portuguesa*. Braga: Faculdade de Filosofia.
de Albuquerque, M. (1993). (with Eduardo Vera Cruz), *Da Igualdade. Introdução à Jurisprudência*. Coimbra: Almedina.
de Almeida Santos, A. (2008). *Que Nova Ordem Mundial?*. Lisbon: Campo da Comunicação.
Aristotle, *Nicomachean Ethics*.
de Baecque, A., & Mélonio, F. (2005). *Lumieres et liberté, Histoire Culturelle de la France, III*. dir.
Debray, R. (2009). À l'ère des people je parle des peuples. *Le Magazine Littéraire.*, *488*, 96.
Debray, R. (2010). *Le moment fraternité*. Paris: Folio.
del Carmen Rovira, M. (1958). *Eclecticos portugueses del siglo XVIII y algunas de sus influencias en America*. México.
de Magalhães-Vilhena, V. (Ed.). (1980). *Utopia e Utopistas Franceses do Século XVIII*. Lisboa: Livros Horizonte.
de Oliveira Ramos, L. A. (1988). *Sob o Signo das 'Luzes'*. Lisbon: Imprensa Nacional – Casa da Moeda.
Denis, C. (2005). *Revive la République*. Paris: Armand Colin.
Dias, J. (1985). *O Essencial sobre os Elementos Fundamentais da Cultura Portuguesa*. Lisboa: Imprensa Nacional-Casa da Moeda.
Didier, B. (1987). *Le siècle des Lumières*. Paris: MA Editions.
Droixhe, D., & Gossiaux, P.-P. (Eds.). (1985). *L'Homme des Lumières et la Découverte de l'autre*. Bruxelles: Editions de l'Université de Bruxelles.
de Jaucourt, C. Grand Seigneur, *Encyclopédie*, org. Diderot/D'Alember, t. XIV.
Dryzek, J. (2000). *Deliberative Democracy and Beyond, Liberal, Critics, Contestation*. Oxford: Oxford University Press.
Dworkin, R. (1977). *Taking Rights seriously*. London: Duckworth.
Ehrhard, J. (1970). *L'Idée de Nature en France a l'Aube des Lumière*. Paris: Flammarion.
Elster, J. (Ed.). (1998). *Deliberative Democracy*. Cambridge: Cambridge University Press.
Eluard, P. (1942). *Liberté. Poésies et verities*. Paris: Minuit.
Fabre, J. (1963). *Lumières et Romantisme*. Paris: Klincksieck.
Ferreira da Cunha, P. (2003). *O Século de Antígona*. Coimbra: Almedina.
Ferreira da Cunha, P. (2005). *Política Mínima* (2nd ed.). Coimbra: Almedina.
Ferreira da Cunha, P. (2008). *Direito Constitucional Anotado*. Lisboa: Quid Juris.
Ferreira da Cunha, P. (2009a). *Geografia Constitucional. Sistemas Juspolíticos e Globalização*. Lisbon: Quid Juris.
Ferreira da Cunha, P. (2009b). *Pensar o Estado*. Lisbon: Quid Juris.
Ferreira da Cunha, P. (2012). *Constituição & Política*. Lisbon: Quid Juris.
Ferreira da Cunha, P. (2014). *La Cour constitutionnelle internationale. Une idée qui fait son chemin*. http://www.carthage.tn/sites/default/files/files/La-Cour-Constitutionnelle-Internationale-ICCo-une-idée-qui-fait-son-chemin.pdf.
Foucault, M. (1993). Qu'est-ce que les Lumières. *Magazine Littéraire*, *309*, 61 et sq.
Garnier. (1974). Lumières et Révolution [special issue]. *Dix-Huitième Siècle*, 6, Paris.
Garnier. (1978). Qu'est-ce que les Lumières [special issue]. *Dix-Huitième Siècle*, 10, Paris.
Goyard-Fabre, S. (1972). *La Philosophie des Lumières en France*. Paris: Klincksieck.
Guérard Latour, S. (2003). *Le Société Juste. Égalité et Différence*, trad. port., *A Sociedade Justa, Igualdade e Diferença*. Porto: Porto Editora.
Guerreiro, S. (2005). *As Fronteiras da Tolerância - Liberdade Religiosa e Proselitismo na Convenção Europeia dos Direitos do Homem*. Coimbra: Almedina.
Gusdorf, G. (1976). *Naissance de la conscience romantique au siècle des Lumières*. Paris: Payot.
Gutman, A., & Thompson, D. (1996). *Democracy and disagreement*. Cambridge, London: The Belknap Press of Harvard University Press.
Hazard, P. (1961). *La Crise de la conscience européenne*. 1680–1715. Paris: Fayard.
Hazard, P. (1979). *La pensée europénne au XVIIIe siècle*. Paris: Fayard.
Herr, R. (1960). *The eighteenth century revolution in Spain*. Princeton: Princeton University Press.
Huisman, B., & Salem, J. (1982). *Les Philosophes et la Liberté*. Paris: Editions Bruno Huisman.

Jaeger, W. (1936). *Paideia, Die Formung des Griechichen Menschen*. Berlin: Walter de Gruyter. Port. transl. by Artur M. Parreira, *Paideia. A Formação do Homem Grego*, Lisboa, Aster, 1979, p. 28.

Jaeger, W. (1979). *Paideia, Die Formung des Griechichen Menschen*, Berlin: Walter de Gruyter, 1936, Port. transl. by Artur M. Parreira, *Paideia. A Formação do Homem Grego*, Lisbon, Aster.

Jam, J.-L. (Ed.). (1992). *Eclectisme et cohérences des Lumières. Mélanges offerts à Jean Ehrard*. Paris: Librairie Nizet.

Kant, I. (1784). *Was ist Aufklärung?*. Berlinische Monatsschrift, pp. 481–494.

La Bruyère. (1688). *Les caractères*, XIV, 15.

Leite Pinto, R. (2006). *Neo-Republicanismo*. Democracia e Constituição, Lisbon: Universidade Lusíada Editora.

Lichtenberger, A. (1895). *Le socialisme au XVIIIe siècle. Etudes sur les idées socialistes dans les écrivains français du XVIIIe siècle, avant la Révolution*. Paris.

Levy-Bruhl, (s.d.). *O Ideal Republicano*, Port. transl., Porto: Renovação Democrátiva.

Lynn, J., & Jay, A. (1984). *Yes Minister*. London.

Lynn, J., & Jay, A. (1986). *Yes Prime Minister*. London.

Montesquieu, *Spicilège*, n.º 525.

Macedo, S. (Ed.). (1999). *Deliberative democracy, essays on democracy and disagreement*. Oxford: Oxford University Press.

Mandeville, B. (1988). *The fable of the bees or private vices, publick benefits*. Indianapolis: Liberty Classics.

Mate, R., & Niewöhner, F. (Eds.). (1989). *La Ilustración en España y Alemania*. Barcelona: Anthropos.

Mauzy, R. (1965). *L'idée du bonheur dans la littérature et la pensée françaises au XVIIIe siècle*. Paris.

Montesquieu (1748) *De l'Esprit des lois*.

Mornet, D. (1989). *Les origines intellectuelles de la Révolution française 1715-1787* (new ed.). Lyon: La Manufacture.

Mortier, R. (1982). *L'Originalité. Une nouvelle catégorie esthétique au siècle des Lumières*. Genève: Droz.

Mousnier, R., & Labrousse, E. (1985). *Le XVIIIe siècle. L'Époque des Lumières (1715-1815)* (6th ed.). Paris: PUF.

Nicolson, H. (1987). A defense of shyness. In: W. E. Williams (Ed.), *A book of english essais*.

Ortega y Gasset, J. (1982). *Historia como Sistema. Mirabeau ou o Político*. Brasília: Editôra Universidade de Brasília.

Petit, P. (2001). *A theory of freedom: From the psychology to the politics of agency*. Cambridge: Polity Press.

Plard, H. (Ed.). (1986). *Morale et Vertu au siècle des Lumières*. Bruxelles: Editions de l'Université de Bruxelles.

Portalis, J.-E.-M. (1820). *De l'usage et de l'abus de l'esprit philosophique durant le XVIIIe siècle*, Paris.

Rawls, J. (1971). *A theory of justice*. Harvard: Harvard University Press.

Reis, A. (2002). Os Valores Republicanos Ontem e Hoje. In A. Reis (Ed.), *A República Ontem e Hoje, II Curso Livre de História Contemporânea*. Colibri: Lisboa.

Ribeiro R. J. (2008). *A República*.

Rocha, A. (2008). *Espírito Santo. Aspectos de uma Pneumatologia Solidária à Condição Humana*. São Paulo: Vida.

Rousseau J.-J. (1762). *Du Contrat social*.

Resta, E. (2002). *Il Diritto Fraterno*. Roma, Bari: Laterza.

Rudé, G. (1972). *Europe in the eighteenth century. Aristocracy and the bourgeois challenge*. London: Weidenfeld and Nicolson.

Santiago Nino, C. (1996). *The constitution of deliberative democracy*. New Haven, London: Yale University Press.

Serra, J. B. (2002). O Republicanismo entre o Ideal e a Realidade. *A República Ontem e Hoje*, pp. 41 et sq.

Sgard, J. et al. (1985). *Lumières et Lueurs du XVIIIe siècle.* 1715–1789. Paris: L'Arbre Verdoyant.

Shaw, B. (1944). *Everybody's political what is what?*. London: Constable.

Sherwin-White, A. N. (2001). *The Roman Citizenship* (2nd ed.). Oxford: Oxford University Press.

Starobinski, J. (1987). *L'Invention de la Liberté* (new ed.). Genève: Editions d'Art Albert Skira.

Starobinski, J. (1988). *1789: Les emblèmes de la raison*. Schwarcz: Companhia das Letras.

Starobinski, J. (1989). *Le remède dans le mal. Critique et légitimation de l'artifice à l'âge des Lumières*. Paris: Gallimard.

Tale, C. (1995). *Lecciones de Filosofía del Derecho*. Córdova: Alveroni.

Todorov, T. (2006). *L'esprit des Lumières*. Paris: Laffont.

Trahard, P. (1931–1933). *La sensibilité révolutionnaire (1789–1794),*. vol. 6 Paris: Boivin et Cie. editeurs.

Trahard, P. (1933). *Les maîtres de la sensibilité française au XVIIIe siècle (1715–1789)*. Paris: Boivin et Cie. editeurs.

Valéry, P. (1945). Fluctuations sur la liberté. *Regards sur le monde actuel.*

Vovelle, M. (Ed.). (1997). *L'Umo del Illuminismo.* Port. transl. By Maria Georgina Segurado, *O Homem do Iluminismo*. Lisboa: Presença.

Willard, N. (1963). *Le génie et la folie au XVIIIe siècle*. Paris: P.U.F.

References

Chapter 4
The European Constitution, a Republican Construction?

El concepto de 'república' se entiende ahora en el sentido de 'libertad', 'democracia' y 'responsabilidad'.

Peter Haeberle, *El Estado Constitucional*, Spanish transl. by Héctor Fix Fierro, Mexico, UNAM, 2003, p. 37.

4.1 Theoretical *Verfremdungseffekt*

The project of the "Treaty that establishes a Constitution for Europe," beyond its political implications, itself poses some challenges to classical constitutional theory. At a first glance, it may seem totally heterodox in light of the current constitutional canons, and therefore in terms of the *pouvoir constituant*. However, a stricter analysis of modern (especially French) constitutional history may detect revealing similarities between modern constitutional codification (the modern constitutionalism, since the eighteenth and nineteenth centuries—but still our common paradigm) and that project, done by the "European Convention," for a European constitution. The formula "treaty" (as it is well known, a category typical of Public International Law) also represents a departure from the normal process of codifying constitutions. But rather than a "constitutional treaty," we shall consider it for the purpose of our study as a true constitution, since although it requires an approval by treaty, in general, it contains the purpose and the substance of a true constitution (for some interpreters, a constitutional chart, not issued from the pure constitutional power… but that is another problem).

But this is to be anticipated. There is a route to be followed before we can eventually arrive at such conclusions—a route that begins in the search for what is unfamiliar to us.

One of the most common forms of coping with the new or the unknown is to think of what it has in common with the old and the known. After theorizing about the known, an attempt is made to integrate what is not known. This procedure, though undoubtedly a cautious one, is itself prone to error. This has to do with

P. Ferreira da Cunha, *Political Ethics and European Constitution*,
SpringerBriefs in Law, DOI 10.1007/978-3-662-45600-2_4

its conservative nature. It risks an enquiry that may pay insufficient attention to predictable events (and to their likely conjugation), over-emphasizing the shock of difference, and forgetting that continuity is possible, at least in part, and not merely a break.

The alternative to this procedure is one that neglects the interpretative mesh of the past and the present, and falls into the opposite error: it does not permit an approach to the known, and as a rule privileges those differences that will not always seem obvious.

However, what is new invariably has its roots in the past. It follows from this that a dialogue must be established as a means of perfecting our knowledge of what is going on.

The European constitution has been seen as either something totally new—a radical change of paradigm (just as European Union Law was itself understood by some as a novel departure from previous Law)—, or, as a gradual continuum, building upon what had already been done in the Maastricht, Amsterdam, and Nice treaties. In both cases, it seems to us that one aspect of reality is being overvalued at the expense of another.

The codified European Constitution tried by the Convention presided over by the former French President Valléry Giscard D'Estaing, as well as the present main constitutional document, the Treaty of Lisbon, has old and new elements, not only in relation to the (uncodified) European Constitution currently in force (always with a written nucleus constituted by the treaty of Nice and what followed it). All this complex evolution therefore represents a good opportunity to evaluate the present-day validity of classical constitutional theory. We therefore turn next to an analysis of the manifold challenges the European Constitution poses to constitutional theory, attempting to review those topics of common concern to both.

4.2 European Constitution and Constitutional Theory

4.2.1 The Two Classical Theories of Constitution

There are many definitions and perspectives of what a Constitution is, a doctrinal tradition which, directly or indirectly, terminated in two formulas that mirror—albeit not clearly or symmetrically—the two great types of Constitution that have always existed.

The first formula makes explicit the historical-universal concept of the Constitution. Although many of its doctrines have been forgotten in practice, there have been very few attempts at general constitutional theory that do not refer to it, at least in abstract terms. This perspective is normally quoted from the formula devised by Lassalle in his famous speech "What is a Political Constitution," and this states, as is well known, that:

> Every country in every age has therefore had a *real* constitution. What is peculiar to modern times is – and it is important always to bear this clearly in mind – not the *actual* but the written constitution – the piece of paper.[1]

The logic of this formula identifies the political community or society with the constitution, and ends in the mythification of merely written code, by which our imaginations are held captive at the most superficial level. Curiously, this myth of a Constitution that is identified with a public Law code goes unmentioned in any of its specific theorizations: it is implicit in a way that does not need to be verbalized.

So, if all countries and ages have a real constitution, a political balance of powers (more or less in equilibrium, which depend on the political/constitutional regime), the first moment in constitutional history is, of course, one of material and not formal constitutions: not codified ones, but living in diverse texts or even unwritten, depending on custom. This kind of constitution has different designations according to the authors. Some underline the unwritten or the material aspect—but it seems that the most important aspect is their natural or historical reality. So, first we had historical or natural constitutions. At least one of those survived: that of the United Kingdom. Not unwritten, as many manuals repeat, because it was written from at least the *Magna Charta* and other ancient documents, but of course not codified even in present days.

But we live, in general, under another constitutional concept. The French *Declaration of Human Rights and Citizens*, of 26 August 1789 (adopted as a Preamble to the first French Constitution codified in 1791), which contains in Article XVI an explicit (and implicit) formulation of the modern codified concept of Constitution: the one of at least a certain voluntarism (constitution is not just "a question of art and time," historically sedimentary). It represents the second major type of Constitution, the second in time and the closest to us chronologically and intellectually speaking.

These combined perspectives make clear that there are two historical phases of constitutionalism. The first period, that of historical constitutionalism, is the natural, gradual, product of a historical evolution, or a "cold" process, to paraphrase Levi-Strauss. The second, that of voluntarism, is mentally designed and generated, codified, and the product of "hot" history—above all, the product of revolutions, beginning with liberal revolutions. Obviously, we will not easily find—or not without a great deal of imagination—a contemporary text relating to the natural or historical phase which invokes the fundamental laws of the kingdom, or its customs or practices, etc. The source of legitimation is the people, and their constituent power.

[1] Lassalle (1862).

4.2.2 The Lesson of the French Declaration of Human Rights and Citizens: Modern Constitutional Requisites

If the requirements of the historical or traditional constitution must be deduced, its fundamentals sought in the testaments of kings, ordinances, practices and conventions reiterated, and also laws, and the fundamental laws of the kingdoms (not only written ones), etc., the requirements of a modern constitution would seem to be more accessible, if only because they belong to a time of expository and written logic.[2] This is, however, only partially true. On one hand, there is some pressure to be explicit, to decide what is necessary to include in the formulation of a Constitution. But, on the other hand, there are elements that will still be missing in the written prescription.

The French *Déclaration* solemnly prescribes:

> Toute société dans laquelle la garantie des droits n'est pas assurée, ni la séparation des pouvoirs déterminée, n'a point de constitution.

This article of the Declaration by itself does not bind us immediately to a written constitutional text as a constitutional requirement. In theory it would be possible to think of a society (and it is merely of a society that the text speaks, and not of a code that prescribes the organization of the *public thing, res publica*) in which rights are guaranteed and powers separated, but one not having a codified juridical instrument, a unique and fundamental written regulator of these things. In this way, the Declaration most often thought to be the starting point of modern constitutionalism could also be considered as the expression of a historical constitutionalism. But in practice, of course, it would not be so considered. This is because the guarantee of rights the article speaks of is not just any guarantee, but one assuring equal rights for all—not, that is to say, prerogatives or privileges ("private laws") conceded to certain social groups or corporations, etc. Until the modern constitutions (and declarations of rights) encoded them, universal rights were unknown as components of a model society. Since the old traditional monarchical power (not the absolutist one) can be described as a "conjugated power,"[3] and if in all societies there is always a balance of and between powers, in the sense we now use the term the separation of powers only fits into this new phase of society and politics.

Not to detain ourselves further on one of the great pillars of modern constitutional theory, we can say, remembering Montesquieu, that a social distribution of powers exists, in which the bourgeoisie (at that time "representative" of the People) is also contemplated, and significantly so. Never before did this type of social distribution exist beyond the purely technical and functional sort that would develop until the sway of the imagination and the doctrine of *ars combinatoria*.

---

[2] Goody (1986).

[3] Botelho (1986), pp. 38 et sq.

All the above suggests that the Declaration we speak of, without actually claiming that fundamental rights and the separation of powers should be necessarily inscribed in a code of political rights, in fact ends by presupposing the three elements: rights, separation of powers, and written political code, i.e., constitution in modern terms. Universal fundamental rights such as these were first coined in those *old* liberal times (and endure today, under other forms), and the separation of powers was first "determined" (the word can suggest a more definitive idea of fixation, and very likely a written one). Since both requirements were settled in Article XVI—this in turn takes us to the juridical-political environment, from which may be deduced unexpressed, albeit fundamental, principles.

Article IV makes it clear that the natural rights of all can only be defined by Law (pre-supposedly written) and in this way brings us closer to the need for a written Constitution as an essential instrument of modern constitutionalism. But the Law in this case emanated from sovereignty. Since the latter was then conceived as a power that resided essentially in the nation, it was only from the nation that the individual derived any concrete exercise of power. In the words of the Article:

> Le principe de toute souveraineté réside essentiellement dans la Nation. Nul corps, nul individu ne peut exercer d'autorité qui n'en émane expressément.

In addition, Article VI establishes (among others) the principles of popular participation and political representation, from which emanates the Law, the key power in constitutionalism, declaring:

> La loi est l'expression de la volonté générale. Tous les citoyens ont droit de concourir personnellement ou par leurs représentants à sa formation. Elle doit être la même pour tous, soit qu'elle protège, soit qu'elle punisse. Tous les citoyens, étant égaux à ses yeux, sont également admissibles à toutes dignités, places et emplois publics, selon leur capacité et sans autre distinction que celle de leurs vertus et de leurs talents.

Therefore, the 1789 French *Declaration of Human Rights and Citizens*, not only in its classic Article XVI, but also as a whole, points to the most relevant traits of modern constitutionalism and the most enlightened aspects of present-day constitutional theory.

First of all, there is the dyad expressed in the article itself: fundamental rights and separation of powers. Thereafter, the constitutional mythic triad emerges from the more general support and the context of the text: to the first two items is implicitly added the sacred text (*sacred instrument*, the Americans will say about their Constitution) of the codified constitution. Furthermore, in the broader perspective of the juridical-political system sketched by the Declaration as a whole, two more traits stand out: the notion of popular/national sovereignty (a sharp distinction is difficult today) and its corollary, the notion of political representation, if not democracy itself.

The informing traits of modern constitutionalism, all of them having their own degrees of myth,[4] are clear. They amount to fundamental rights (based on natural

[4] *V.g.* Ferreira da Cunha (2002).

rights, and enlarged internationally for the most part as human rights); the separation (and interdependency) of powers; the sacrosanct text of the codified constitution; and the concepts of popular/national sovereignty, representation, and democracy (or sovereignty and democracy identified as representation). These are the salient traits of modern constitutionalism.

4.2.3 European Constitution, Natural Constitution, and Codified Constitution

The dice having been thrown, it would not seem a difficult task to frame the European Constitution. But before that, an important distinction must be made. We can talk about several European constitutions, divided in accordance with the classic *magna divisio*, and more to the point, in terms of what divides them from each other. Before the European Convention a natural, historically-evolved European Constitution had come into being, shaped by treaties, conventions, jurisprudence, and even with elements of the national constitutions of the member states, etc. If the Convention's project had been approved, we would have now a modern, codified, European Constitution, although with a strange designation, and a bizarre manner of creation and approval. But the French and Dutch veto aborted that attempt.

The still current, naturally evolved European Constitution poses an interesting challenge to constitutional theory. Although it is natural, it is still imbued with the concepts of fundamental rights, some separation of powers, some representative aspects, democracy and, in a theoretical sense at least, the "sovereignty" *hoc* sensu of European citizens. While it is uncodified, it is, however, written and very much written—scattered in multiple documents. The Treaty of Lisbon, reassembles many of the Convention's text and proposals, and functions as the main written basis. Would it change a lot if it was baptized as a real "European Constitution"?

With the proposed codified texts to replace the historical constitution of Europe, the juridical dimension of fundamental rights becomes clearer, inasmuch as the Charter of European Rights is incorporated, although the judiciary, even without this *démarche*, obviously would not refrain from applying them as a real constitutional text. And it did very well.

In what concerns the remaining aspects, there are in the text of the Convention changes that affect all the member states, though the observer's perspectives will differ. For some, for example, there will be greater separation of powers, for others not so; for some, more representation, for others, less. It is difficult to speak apodictically of this new reality, tracing the complex threads of existing and proposed powers, checks and balances, not to mention those divergent ideological perspectives that will likely complicate it in diametrically opposed ways.

At the time, it seemed to us that the separation of powers (*sui generis*) of the new Constitution—if the President of the European Council and the Ministry of

Foreign Affairs do not assume excessively proactive roles—would be reinforced. Namely, the intervention of national parliaments in the legislative procedure, though discrete, would attend to that. The European Parliament reinforces itself, chiefly, and significantly (its symbolic strength being due to emphasizing its democratic dimension), through the new legislation process, a form of "co-decision" in which the participation of the Commission and Parliament is always claimed. As Montesquieu might have put it, there is a requirement to proceed in concert (*aller de concert).*[5]

But now, from the practice of the Treaty of Lisbon, we are not so sure. For example, the end of budget sovereignty of national parliaments seems to be a very complex reality, not of classical separation of powers, but of checks and balances between large rich countries on one side, and small poor ones on the other. Also the insistence of some to make the national constitutions have a deficit limit in their constitutions seems to us that *institutionnalists* have no idea about the meaning and functions of a constitution. No excessive deficit is allowed by any reasonable material constitution, but of course this is an obvious consequence of many principles, and of the constitutional essence of good government. And by no means would the simple inclusion of an article about that change anything about the reality of indebtedness. Again, it is a question of the particular politicians who govern, their values and virtues (and among these their competence and political common sense—much overlooked these days), not of constitutional engineering.

This reinforcement of the European Parliament calls for more representative legitimacy, a broader extension of what we could call, very anachronically, the "European sovereignty" of European citizens. It is true that to speak of "European sovereignty" at a moment when the concept of sovereignty is itself in crisis, makes matters more complicated. But the truth is that, in many ways the new architecture and the new constitutional mechanics point to a reinforcement of the principle of popular representation—giving the demographic factor a weight that may compensate for the much-criticized democratic *deficit* of the European constitutions. This consideration can affect, to the point that some think is dangerous, the representation of the member states and their notional "equality" (which is nevertheless, in principle, a cornerstone of the Union). On this point negative arguments converge from both sides of the critical spectrum: from *souverainistes* and Eurosceptics to federalists. One side argues, along with the principle of more or less engagement, for the preservation of national sovereignty. The other side declines to see in European institutions any truly federal organ, directly representative of equality within the union, of peoples and states. They see instead the numerical dominance of large countries over smaller ones. But this is another problem... One might say, *mutatis mutandis*: for some the cup is almost full, for some others it is almost empty.

[5] Montesquieu (1748), XI, 6.

The European codified Constitution has, in comparison with national codified constitutions, a problem of some delicacy. A national constitution can to a certain extent count on the historical ballast, often of centuries, for a given sociological identity, certain equilibrium of forces, and normative representations. The European Constitution, being supranational, cannot so easily implant itself in a European social and historical reality having itself such a short history of democratic integration dating only from the Second World War. This means that it may be relatively easy to evaluate the adequacy and the normative strength of a national codified constitution, mediating a compromise between the balance-constitution and the program-constitution. But where there are no pre-existing European people or a socially grounded "pan-"European reality, the European codified Constitution represents a very daring act of voluntarism, and will inevitably sacrifice much more to pragmatism. Consequently, such a codification, which is important because it answers the need for certainty, security, order, simplification, etc. (particularly at a time when what is not written and not publicized is easily ignored), ends up by becoming quite plastic, permitting both a laxity of compliance and the competition of several utopias. The codified European Constitution (even in the current low profile version in juridical terms, the Treaty of Lisbon) in this way represents a return of the utopian ideal that nourished the political imagination in the eighteenth century, and inspired the written European constitutions…both by direct influence and by reaction.

4.2.4 European Constitution and Constituent Power

Alexander Hamilton, writing about judicial power, made an approach to the idea of constituent power, even if not to its actual expression:

> There is no position which depends on clearer principles, than that every act of a delegated authority, contrary to the tenor of the commission under which it is exercised, is void. No legislative act, therefore, contrary to the Constitution, can be valid. To deny this, would be to affirm, that the deputy is greater than his principal; that the servant is above his master; that the representatives of the people are superior to the people themselves; that men acting by virtue of powers, may do not only what their powers do not authorize, but what they forbid.[6]

In the same way d'Holbach, in his Encyclopedia article *Représentants*, comes close, although the constituents of whom he talks are merely electors: "les représentants supposent des constituants de qui leur pouvoir est émané".

The idea of representation is present in both of them, but only Sieyes articulates its dynamic principle and is certain about modern constitutionalism. When, in his classic, *Qu'est-ce que le tiers état* (written in 1788 and published in the following year) the Abbot advances the idea of constituent power, we do not know if he was

6 Hamilton (1788).

aware that he was coining a basic concept of modern constitutionalism (perhaps of all constitutionalism, *mutatis mutandis*), or if the expression emerged from his pen in the heat of political battle. Whatever the reason, let us recall that his founding words, like those of the Declaration of Rights in 1789, constitute a "sacred" text:

> La nation existe avant tout, elle est l'origine de tout. Sa volonté est toujours légale, elle est la loi elle-même. Avant elle et au-dessus d'elle il n' y a que le droit naturel. Si nous voulons nous former une idée juste de la suite des lois positives qui ne peuvent émaner que de sa volonté, nous voyons en première ligne les lois constitutionnelles, qui se divisent en deux parties: les unes règlent l'organisation et les fonctions du corps législatif; les autres déterminent l'organisation et les fonctions des différents corps actifs. Ces lois sont dites fondamentales, non pas en ce sens qu'elles puissent devenir indépendantes de la volonté nationale, mais parce que les corps qui existent et agissent par elles ne peuvent point y toucher. Dans chaque partie, la constitution n'est pas l'ouvrage du pouvoir constitué, mais du pouvoir constituant. Aucune sorte de pouvoir délégué ne peut rien changer aux conditions de sa délégation. C'est en ce sens que les lois constitutionnelles sont fondamentales.[7]

This connection of the constituent power to the nation is often invoked as one of the obstacles to defining the European Constitution as a true constitution. There are even those, like Sieyes, who no longer talk of a nation, but speak of a State. It is incomprehensible that a State that is constituted and not constituent could replace the Nation. It would be easier to admit a Europe constituted not as a nation but of nations, not of one people but of peoples. We believe that we can speak of a European constituent power already in the Convention. A power undoubtedly maculated and imperfect, as Sieyes recognized in respect of the constituent power of the first French codified constitution, and for that reason, lacking in some legal refinements still to come. Let us remember his own words:

> Les représentants de la nation française, réunis en Assemblée nationale, reconnaissent qu'ils ont par leurs mandats la charge spéciale de régénérer la Constitution de l'État. En conséquence ils vont, à ce titre, exercer le pouvoir constituant, et pourtant, comme la représentation actuelle n'est pas rigoureusement conforme à ce qu'exige une telle nature de pouvoir, ils déclarent que la Constitution qu'ils vont donner à la nation, quoique provisoirement obligatoire pour tous, ne sera définitive, qu'après qu'un nouveau pouvoir constituant, extraordinairement convoqué pour cet unique objet, lui aura donné un consentement que réclame la rigueur des principes.[8]

The austerity of these principles contrasts with the self-satisfaction of the Convention delegates. In the Preamble, they congratulate themselves upon the elaboration of the Constitution.

Actually, the situation is in every respect similar to the French one. The delegates to the Convention (the source of all subsequent constitutional steps) have constituency power, although rather imperfect. The ideal solution, perhaps, would have been to call for a European constituency assembly, a European Parliament with constituent powers, whose work would later be submitted to the equivalent of a

---

[7] Sieyes (1789a), p. 68.

[8] Sieyes (1789b/1989), p. 1005.

second chamber (composed of equal numbers of representatives from each one of the European states)—and not just an intergovernmental conference. This solution would have prevented the referendum crisis that blocked the situation in Ireland.

And what happened there was considered very critically by the anti-Europeans, as an example of the lack of democracy in the European constructions: they say that the Irish would be obliged to make so much referenda as necessary to reach to a "Yes" vote. They exaggerate a lot, of course. But it is an argument able to persuade many people in public opinion. And even more so in countries such as Portugal, where a referendum about European integration was never held. European enthusiasts have certain difficulties in dealing with such arguments.

The current invocation of "constituent power" can still provoke implicit criticism of and even outright rebellion against a codified Constitution, which is in fact very difficult to revise. In this way, *mutatis mutandis*, we might be reminded of the thesis of Sieyes in *Qu'est-ce que le Tiers Etat?*

> il serait ridicule de supposer la nation liée elle-même par la Constitution à laquelle elle a assujetti ses mandataires. Non seulement la nation n'est pas soumise à une Constitution, mais elle ne peut pas l'être, mais elle ne doit pas l'être, ce qui équivaut encore à dire qu'elle ne l'est pas.[9]

In consonance with this, Article 28 of the Constitution of 24 June 1793 would also argue that:

> un peuple a toujours le droit de revoir, de réformer et de changer sa Constitution. Une génération ne peut assujettir à ses lois les générations futures.

To which we might add Abott's thoughts about the rights of the Men and the Citizen in the passage referred to above:

> (…) la Constitution d'un peuple n'est et ne peut être que la Constitution de son gouvernement, et du pouvoir chargé de donner des lois, tant au peuple qu'au gouvernement. Une Constitution suppose avant tout un pouvoir constituant.[10]

In our opinion, a European proto-constituent power has been expressed. In an important conference on the European Constitution, we asked (of course *cum grano salis*) a prestigious member of the Convention about the eventual intervention of the Holy Spirit in it. He seemed not only to agree with this as a possibility, but dwelt also on parallels with the French constituency situation. That proto-constituent power invalidates the rigor that manifests itself in the case of Nations and surprisingly—of States. But we believe that it needs improvement, since actually many institutions of power (see the studies on violence in the genesis of politics[11]) are born with some defects.

---

[9] Sieyes (1789a), p. 69.

[10] Sieyes (1789b/1989), p. 1013.

[11] Girard (1978, 1972).

4.2.5 European Constitution: Treaty or Constitution?

Are we to speak of a Treaty, Constitution, or a hybrid *tertium genus*, "constitutional treaty"? To paraphrase, *mutatis mutandis*, an apt remark attributed to Saint Jerome, '...in the letters of the names dances destiny...' Not only is the fate of this project inherent in its diverse designation, but also the perspective of the observers (and sometimes of their education or profession, namely their academic profession). The sheer contrariety of opinion is eloquent testimony to that fact.

Usually critics of the "alleged" European constitution, the "so-called" European constitution, or the "pseudo-"European constitution, hold in general that what we have is *merely a treaty*. And they may evoke its own name: Treaty of Lisbon. According to this argument, the denomination of "constitution" is clearly unreasonable: an attempt to label what is actually an association of States as if it was one single State, federation, federal state, or "super-"European State. The expression "constitution" is above all objectionable to those who associate Constitution with a national State, and to those who are committed to a greater or lesser degree of "sovereignty," the reason being that the European Union must only be an association of States, and characterize the various shades of federalism as "deviations."

On the other hand, when the constitutional aspect of the designation is emphasized, it may imply a hope on the part of those who favor the term (not always consciously recognized) of greater integration, namely some sort of federalism. But, above all, what is emphasized (and criticized) in this perspective is the prospect of a greater autonomy for European institutions rather than a mere intergovernmental understanding, a long way from any diffuse reminiscence of the classic International Law ruling over the Union.

Nevertheless, that same International Law, before the advent of positive international law, with its corollary that "no law, no judge and no police" (*ni loi, ni juge, ni gendarme*) couldn't obviate traditional "gunboat diplomacy". In fact, a kind of war... But it supposed a *Grundnorm* of the jus naturale kind or at least a general principle following Hans Kelsen's in his classical *Reine Rechtslehre*[12]: *pacta sunt servanda*. And for Afonso Queiró, this lack of a *ius scriptum* sourced in international law would be supplied by a new norm "immanent of the international community," which for him should be termed "constitutional" or "fundamental."[13] The general idea of "constitution" attaches thus to more profound notions of essentiality or fundamentality, so that, for example, in the field of historical-juridical doctrine, the history of International Law embraces the history of Constitutional Law. In fact, we would feel tempted to say that it embraces what is *materially constitutional*, essential in the general foundations of other branches of law. We cannot forget the idea of a constitutional history which is broader than a history of constitutional law, as we may learn in Otto Brunner.[14] Thus, between

[12] Kelsen (2008), new edition.

[13] Rodrigues Queiró (1975), col. 1897.

[14] Brunner (1939/1992, 1949, 1956, 1978).

International Law and Constitutional Law, it is always possible to build interesting bridges and dialogues. The idea of the International Constitutional Court is now one of the laboratories of confluence between these two fields.

But our question here is different. On the basis of the dichotomy of perspectives and the duality of experiences referred to above, everything seems to indicate that whoever accepts the *historical-universal concept of the constitution* would thereby have to admit that the defined political space we call the European Union has a Constitution, irrespective of its juridical-political qualification (and also the international community). This is the *natural and material constitution* of the European Union. In the face of this axiom, it is difficult to deny that a juridical instrument voted to reform, to give order and coherence to the set of scattered norms about power, its structure, means, and ends must in the end be considered materially and substantially, as nothing less than a Constitution, and in these terms, a codified Constitution. So, the Treaty of Lisbon is a constitution in a way replacing another constitution. Of course it would be easier and clearer if the text was called simply "European Constitution," even if approved, in a distorted way, by a treaty, of Lisbon or elsewhere. By the simple fact that a codified Constitution replaces the historical, natural, scattered constitution that we already have, it is possible to reach the qualification of the new *quid*.

The fact that the treaty is the juridical form of European Constituition's legal realization is related, not to the substantial nature, the material or content of what is approved (that is constitutional—as was the case with previous treaties, though with more *lacunae* in the legal detail concerning the material constitutional space), but rather to the European tradition of deepening the Union by following this path. The European Union is used to treaties, so let us make another one, but this time it was "the" one…

However, as we can see by the refusal of France and the Netherlands, the method raises many more problems than the normal procedure, which would have involved convoking a more representative Convention or a European Parliament with constituency powers. This, working in tandem with a second Convention equally representative of the intervening States, would have concluded the text of the Constitution with no major problems. A process such as this could perhaps have prevented democratic/representative purist criticisms—some of which were very convincing. In any case, the form of a treaty is not in vain. It would imply the unanimity of participants from the beginning—at least in principle and for the internal perfection of the treaty.

Whoever defends the idea of a European Constitution cannot help feeling a bitter disappointment in the face of some decisions the Convention made with so little democratic input, however informed by constitutionalist *élan*. It seems to be almost the same disappointment we feel about those other decisions left to conventiclers, of strict agreements among the heads of government and State (who seem sometimes to have been little animated with the unity of the European spirit), of nationalist or selfish groups, or the obstructionism of intergovernmental consensus. Even referendums, with concentration of negative feelings—*coincidentia oppositorum*—seem to have been subverted in their nature.

In some sense, the European Convention delegates are, in this process, the most defrauded of all—and are those who, nevertheless, mythically seem to smile serenely at everybody while pushing the train that now goes so slowly up the historical hill. If not down…

4.2.6 Constitutional Treaty

Usually, like those who defend the expression "treaty," *tout court*, those who use the term "constitutional treaty" look for a minimalist form to avoid the underlying danger of "federalism." Others who use the expression disregard all that and, in a quite different sense, hope to cushion the shock of the new (*Verfrendungseffekt*); after all it would be "just" a constitutional treaty. Finally, there are those who use the expression apparently out of a purist concern for accuracy: after all, is not the title of the project in fact the "Treaty that establishes a Constitution for Europe"? Nonetheless, these simple purisms ought not to be taken at face value; we seldom find naivety in these matters… although it is not vain to remember these historic aspects…

Curiously enough, the opposite statement has not been advanced. Because when we talk about a constitutional treaty we look for a middle term, and underlying the formal aspect, for a treaty whose constitutional contents are also specified. It would perhaps be more adequate, in face of the vicissitudes of the method actually found, to speak of the Constitution-treaty. But especially to point out with some rigor the vicissitudes through which a Constitution has to pass if it is to surrender itself to the requirements of a treaty. A *contradictio in terminis* is, in both cases, an obvious risk. In opposition to the term "constitutional treaty," we might argue that all treaties must be constitutional, because they are contracted according to constitutions, and, if they are not, they will be unconstitutional. Other theoretical objections could also be raised. But, of course, one may observe a certain fallacy in our previous statement.

Deep down, everything reverts to the old European democratic deficit, grounded specifically in excessive governmental power (especially from the German–French duet, some say) and a lack of authentic federalization. What results from a constitutional-treaty is, to a large extent, a fundamental text that depends not on the citizens of a political society as a whole (without even much dependence on the demographic weight of each member state: that would be the lesson of the *volonté générale* in Rousseau), but on the agreements of States. And even when, following the defective process, the dissatisfaction of citizens expresses itself in a "no"-vote, it is not the citizens that interpret such dissatisfactions, nor even the European Parliament that represents them, but once again the simple operation of intergovernmental work.

We can understand that it would be insensitive to treat the member states, lords of a long and sometimes painful and bloody history of independence, like the United States of America, establishing a majority ratification process for a Constitution.

This would take insufficient account of the popular will, mainly in the States that in such a process would eventually say "no". The method of the treaty had the advantage of taking into account all the positions in presence. And we must understand that unanimity is very important for any future constitutional dispensation, when the Peoples of Europe will decide to create a European Federation. For now, a utopia, we admit. And it seems very very far away these days.

Although unanimity always runs the risk of national selfishness, the failure of the European summit of 17 June 2005, after a double rejection, represented a drawback in the intergovernmental sense. Not only was the Constitution put in a drawer, a type of postponement that suggests a failure of leadership, but the budget was blocked, despite the lessons in Europeanism given by the new member states, for cohesion's sake. If a Europe of bureaucrats was a danger to be taken into account, a Europe of selfishness means only a denial of Europe. And if a new financial agreement reached in December 2005 allowed the *institutionnalists* to breathe again, nothing new was said about the Constitution…

And so we arrive at a paradox of paradoxes: the formal and codified Constitution that was supposed to be such an act of voluntarism that touching it, in Giscard D'Estaing′s words, would be to open a Pandora's Box, is condemned now to become a ghost Constitution, haunting the past and latent in whatever will be the future. Existing in the shadow of a new treaty, the Treaty of Lisbon, and especially under the normative strength of facts, are the European real politics, a real constitution. We always have the danger that written constitutions, when superficial governments don't pay much attention to them, become like Lassalle's sheets.

4.3 On the Rupture and What It Means for Constitutional Theory

Not every perspective, opinion, or system concerning the Constitution and constitutionalism can be considered a part of Constitutional Theory, much less in being a statistical, archivist, or formalist vision about the "constitution" itself. There are, among the various constitutional theories, those that are authentic (and denounce that human authenticity, for that same reason less contingent) esteemed, valued, ideological bonds,[15] that can neither be contested nor evaded, at the risk of not understanding what we are talking about anymore.

The *ideal concept of constitution* cannot fail to be connected with bourgeois idiosyncrasy (may we remember Carl Schmitt's *Verfassungslehre*?[16]). And sometimes we fear that the development of historical constitutionalism, luckily today an object of

[15] Saldanha (2000), p. 9.

[16] Schmitt (1928).

objective study, has sometimes been used as a "scientific argument" for traditionalist political positions. Any political doctrine can and perhaps should draw inspiration from historical legacies which are more likely to lend it some borrowed glory. The problem is always that of a history that is distorted to serve the ambitions of some at any present.

Besides these theories of the Constitution, old or new, classical or progressive, it seems to us that there may exist today a theoretical nucleus about what makes a Constitution, an essential or ontological constitutional theory. It was only in relation to this nucleus that we have attempted to raise some problems. We have deliberately not touched upon the new tendencies in constitutional theory in the semiotic, symbolic, linguistic, literary, logical, and rhetorical fields as well as those that invite sociological, psychological, economic approaches, etc. We have also excluded the important comparison of the European Constitution with the problem of the State and its theory. This is a subject for another study. But obviously we see that both the traditional elements of the State and its classic purposes are in crisis in face of the novelty of the European Constitution.

During the controversy of the "New Code of Public Law," one of the biggest theoretical constitutional quarrels ever to have occurred in Portugal, Queen Maria I, who initiated the reforms, thought it was necessary to proceed very carefully with the alterations she intended to make to the *Philippine Ordinations* ("Ordenações Filipinas"). This was so that the older counsellors of the Supreme Court, facing so many new norms, would not feel overwhelmed and, unable to adjust to the new methods (even if they were recognisably better), and bring about the noisy collapse of the entire *Desembargo do Paço.*[17] The caution of the Queen became a cause for bitter criticisms.[18] Constitutional theory faced with normative novelties should give us similar pause for thought. The European Constitution should be wary of falling into the same mistake, no matter how excellent we think it may be. And if it is noxious to run uncritically after every novelty, as increasingly is the case, we, as professors and makers of doctrine, no matter how we might honor noble perspectives and familiar certainties, ought not to despise what poses a challenge to our theoretical orthodoxies. The first tendency in the face of novelty is anathema. It is difficult to cope with the breach, and to adapt to a new paradigm. But the second tendency is the precisely opposite: the move toward a more inclusive theory of the constitutional phenomenon, even one that is apparently fractured as a result. Out of this breach we advance to a more comprehensive constitutional theoretical system. *There are more things (…), Horatio…*

[17] *Apud* Delgado da Silva (1828), pp. 162 et sq.

[18] Freire de Mello (1822), p. 96, n. 45.

References

Botelho, A. (1986). Monarquia Poder Conjugado. *Revista Portuguesa de Filosofia do Direito e do Estado* (Vol. 2, pp. 38 *et sq.*).

Brunner, O. (1939/1992). *Land und Herrschaft: Grundfragen der territorialen Verfassungsgeschichte Südostdeutschlands im Mittelalter*. Baden-bei-Wien: Veröffentlichungen des Instituts für Geschichtsforschung und Archivwissenschaft. In Wien. (H. Kaminsky & J. Van Horn Melton, Trans.). *Land and Lordship: Structures of Governance in Medieval Austria*. Philadelphia: University of Pennsylvania Press.

Brunner, O. (1949). *Adeliges Landleben und europäischer Geist. Leben und Werk Wolf Helmhards von Hohber* (pp. 1612–1688). Salzburg: Otto Müller.

Brunner, O. (1956). *Neue Wege der Sozialgeschichte. Vorträge u. Aufsätze*. Göttingen: Vandenhoeck & Ruprecht.

Brunner, O. (1978). *Sozialgeschichte Europas im Mittelalter*. Göttingen: Vandenhoeck & Ruprecht.

Delgado da Silva, A. (1828). *Collecção da Legislação Portuguesa desde a última compilação das ordenações redigida pelo desembargador...* (Legislation from 1775 to 1790). Lisboa: n.p.

Ferreira da Cunha, P. (2002). *Teoria da Constituição. I. Mitos, Memórias. Conceitos*. Lisbon/São Paulo: Verbo.

Freire de Mello, F. (1822). *Discurso sobre delictos e penas* (2nd ed.). Lisboa: n.p.

Girard, R. (1972). *La violence et le sacré*. Paris: Grasset.

Girard, R. (1978). *Des choses cachées depuis la fondation du monde*. Paris: Grasset.

Goody, J. (1986). *The Logic of Writing and the Organisation of Society*. Cambridge: Cambridge University Press.

Hamilton, A. (1788). *The Federalist*, N. 78.

Kelsen, H. (2008). *Reine Rechtslehre: Einleitung in die rechtswissenschaftliche Problematik* (new ed.). Amsterdam: Scientia Verlag.

Lassalle, F. (1862). *Über Verfassungswesen*, (Trans.). On the Essence of Constitutions, conference. Retrieved April 16, 1862 from http://www.marxists.org/history/etol/newspape/fi/vol03/no01/lassalle.htm Original German Text from http://www.gewaltenteilung.de/lassalle.htm.

Montesquieu, (1748). *De l'Esprit des lois*. XI, 6.

Rodrigues Queiró, A. (1975). *Tratado*. In *Verbo – Enciclopédia Luso-Brasileira de Cultura* (Vol. XVII, col. 1897). Lisbon/ São Paulo: Verbo.

Saldanha, N. (2000). *Formação da Teoria Constitucional* (2nd ed.). Rio de Janeiro/São Paulo: Renovar.

Schmitt, C. (1928). *Verfassungslehre*. Berlin: Duncker & Humblot.

Sieyes, E. (1789), Qu'est-ce que le Tiers Etat? Edme Champion ed., p. 68, apud http://visualiseur.bnf.fr/Visualiseur?Destination=Gallica&O=NUMM-89685, electronic ed., 1997.

Sieyes, E. (1789/1989). Reconnaissance et exposition raisonnée des droits de l'Homme et du Citoyen. In: F. Furet & R. Halevi (Eds.), *Orateurs de la Révolution française. I. Les Constituants*. Paris: Gallimard, La Pléiade.

Chapter 5
Global Crisis and European Constitution

Those who would give up essential freedom to purchase a little temporary safety, deserve neither liberty nor safety.

Benjamin Franklin—*Motu* of the book *An Historical Review of the Constitution and Government of Pennsylvania* (1859).

5.1 Trying to Make a Codified Constitution for Europe

In 2000, 2 years before the opening of the European Convention that begun to discuss the problem (February 2002), a dark blue book called "The European Constitution" was published. And there was neither a mistake nor any fraud about it. The subtitle in the cover gave us precisely what we get inside: "Constitutive Treaties and Jurisprudence."[1]

The attempt of the so-called "European Convention" (also called "Convention on the Future of Europe") to make a treaty-constitution (a treaty instituting a constitution for Europe), created the proposal of a strange *tertium genus*, in appearance. But, essentially, it was the project of a new constitution for Europe (which already had, as we know, an historical one). The new text would be not a dispersed constitution as it was before, but a codified one. As it is well known, the French and Dutch *referenda* aborted the process after which the question was wisely postponed, and then some years later the "legacy" of the European Convention, through negotiations among the European government representatives, arrived at a new text. It was quieter and wiser in what concerns the constitutional affirmation, but it is still a Constitution, and its background still has the ideas (and even text) of the first attempt of a European constitutional code. So, the formal European Constitution exists, known as the Treaty of Lisbon.

---

[1] Pereira-Menaut et al. (2000).

P. Ferreira da Cunha, *Political Ethics and European Constitution*,
SpringerBriefs in Law, DOI 10.1007/978-3-662-45600-2_5

5.2 Problems of a Real European Constitution

Of course that is the formal constitution. We should also speak about a material constitution and a real constitution, as general constitutional theory teaches.

This is what we see everyday on TV news: the concrete relations of power in Europe, where all countries and peoples are equal, but some seem to be more equal than others (to remember George Orwell's *Animal farm* pigs refrain). The creation of the expression PIGS or PIIGS (which in itself is a scandal of xenophobia), and the shock of the European establishment when, in the beginning of November 2011, the Greek Prime minister Georgios Papandreo announced a referendum, are very real manifestations of the fears expressed by many true Europeanists when the Conventional Constitution was in progress. Not only radical sovereignists had doubts about the process.

First of all, the fear of creating not a federal Europe (that would be excellent) but of a Europe in which the neoliberalism ruled and the southern countries suffer "austerity" because of the crisis. That, along with political blame and almost religious guilt: a curious and obscure process of stigmatization, the creation of a scapegoat for European problems, mistakes, and so on. That real constitution in Europe (the real exercise of power) is a real problem for Europe. And it is not one that is in the treaties. As always, politics and power are forcing the juridical component of the constitution.

When some people talk of reforming the treaty of Lisbon, it is unfortunately not for the purpose of bringing the European institutions more federalism, which would mean strengthening the co-responsibility of all the peoples and countries, but, on the contrary, a means of making the de facto balance of powers a normative reality, too.

It is indeed curious to remark that, in general, all the de facto power situations aim to legitimate their *statu quo* in juridical terms, normally by changing the previous constitutions. It would be very shocking and outrageous to many national feelings to create a juridical order that might deprive Greeks from their right to make a referendum on their own future (even if we have great reticence to any referendum) ... But when, for instance, rumors spread ideas of putting the flags of European debtors at half mast in European institutions, that says a lot about the European constitutional feelings of some people, and about their constitutional culture. It is not a simple question. When we see the hostility against the presumed lazy debtors (who work and contribute more than the 'rich', as explained in a short but eloquent film by prof. Marcello Rebelo de Sousa[2]), from another side and by the desperate claims of others, we don't get a favorable impression about culture and education nowadays. And this misrepresentation by others in Europe seems to

---

2 http://www.youtube.com/watch?v=dt1wW1zge5E.

be not only a problem, but also a problem that some seemingly don't want to solve. But among all the despair and fear, we still have some positive points, which leads us to the question of the material constitution of Europe.

5.3 The Material Constitution

5.3.1 More European Hope and Imagination

If a national constitution were a "question of art and time," and, although people are divided by antagonistic ideologies, it may have some core matters about which the people of a state may largely agree, we wouldn't be so optimistic about the European common constitutional ideas. The practice of European leaders in recent years, always sailing with the shores in close sight, with no hope, no vision, no courage, giving contradictory signs, manifesting irresolution and fear, hasn't strengthened the trust of Europeans in Europe. The way Europe is dealing with the continuous financial crises is real proof.

So, the prestige of European institutions is not based on calling up passions. The appeals to Europeans to love Europe need to be supported on other foundations. Real ones.

This is not the Europe we dream of. But if this sad, plasticized, and gray Europe has no support in the soul and spirit of Europeans, we think we are not far from the truth claiming that the severe crisis that the European common people are suffering (with the martyrdom of Greeks—and Portuguese and Spanish are next ...) even among more idealistic and distracted people it is creating a strong conscience of things.

Some aspects of the material constitution seem to be reinforced in the general axiological juridical conscience. Of course, a constitution like that (at least in many aspects) fails its application (on the contrary, it is nowadays largely "utopist") in fact: the material constitution is against the real one.

It seems that the crises has supressed many people. Because it is the common people that suffer, not the abstract entities of Banks or Markets nor, of course, the rich (who are, at least, real people ...), who are becoming richer all over the world according to the official numbers. It is a long story. It is said that Margaret Thatcher herself (a guru of neoliberalism in her time) tried to advise the French President François Mitterand:

> Vous n'y pensez pas, François, il n'y a pas assez de grandes fortunes chez vous pour que cela vous rapporte suffisament; taxez les pauvres, ils sont tellement plus nombreux!.[3]
>
> Si non è vero ...

[3] *Apud* Mitterrand (2007), p. 375.

5.3.2 People, Not Only Finance

The first thing to be understood is that the lives of people cannot be in the hands of finance. Finance should not lead politics. And a couple of non-European rating agencies should not decide in the last instance about the life and death of European people. It is urgent that Europe regains it sovereignty, and for that someone needs to make the first move. The problem is whether Europe still has some leeway, or if she is completely submissive to the international shadows (we do not know, for instance, who those emphatically called "markets" really are). It seems tragically absurd, but markets and stock ratings are abstractions, and people's lives are real.

In order to regain sovereignty, Europe may not have a dominant country (or two or even three), or a director, but must be truly federal: each state one vote, each state one voice. And in some difficult matters, of course, a "veto". If we have the problem of so called *blackmail* from some countries, not to compromise is worse. There is no other way of having Justice (and Freedom) in Europe. And the institutions need to adapt to new federal rules at all levels.

At the international level, the Vatican[4] (and the archbishop of Canterbury seemed to agree some days later) called for a general regulation and not the present chaos of anarchic capitalism. Pope Francis, with *Evangelii Gaudium*, underlined the social doctrine of Catholic Church in a very clear way. Some others talk about a "humanist capitalism" as a future solution. It is mainly a question of words and concepts. But many already agree that the situation of speculation and deregulation must stop, and Europe (for the sake of herself and for the sake of the World) must end her vulnerability with strong common politics, really common and really for the general benefit.

5.3.3 Republican Aims

The second material constitutional matter was troubled at the time of the European Convention, and the interpretation of the texts divided even French socialists. But it is clear now to people from many sides of the political rainbow that the present formal European constitution (the Treaty of Lisbon), having inherited the main basis from its predecessor texts, isn't enough to be a guarantee against the raising of neoliberalism, and its practical avatars. Many suspected as much, but others calmed the more skeptical. Now it is clear that the texts, while maybe not intrinsically neoliberal (but that doesn't really matter a lot) are not in practice a sufficient barrier against the law of the jungle.

Agitation of all kinds is expected. Strange movements arising in Europe, meetings of the outraged, suicides, and a general cloudy situation, too many signs already make it very clear that the older order is finishing. But, on the other hand, in social

---

[4] Pontifical Council for Justice and Peace, *Towards reforming the international financial and monetary systems in the context of global public authority*: http://www.justpax.it/eng/home_eng.html.

and economic terms, there seems to be a large consensus among the victims of the jungle law of this system. Even here the leitmotiv of the Republic is a way of translating different aspirations. People agree that politics must have ethics, no longer a commonplace for corruption and hidden games behind the curtains. That is one of the strong meanings of Republic. People don't give up political representation and classic democracy: that is also a Republican feature; and a very important one against all the enemies of democracy who are waiting for their chance.

5.3.4 Social European Model: The Social State

People also interiorized another element of the European way of life, the social European model. The model is being questioned now, not only in theory by the neoliberals, but in practice, everyday, by the restrictive measures of many governments, especially those of the countries under attack of a speculative international plot.

It is thus now possible to affirm that there is a strong element in the European material constitution: the Social State. Not, of course, as we already said, the collectivist or communist state, but that level of civilization in which almost every political family (only neoliberals apart) agree: the traditionalist (mainly monarchists and even absolutists), the conservative, the democratic Christians, even the old liberals, the social liberals, the social-democrats, the labor parties adepts, the democratic socialists, ecologists, new leftists of different roots, and even (certainly *faute de mieux* to their views), far to the left, all the others (communists and radicals of all colors).

The Social State is the social and economic material constitution of Europe, and, of course, any attempt to abolish it is a severe and dangerous unconstitutionality (or anti-constitutionality). And not only an unconstitutional act at the material level, but also at the formal one, because some European national constitutions have the Welfare state explicit in their texts.

Of course some well-thinking hyperrealists should say that it was that same order of things that led us to the borders of financial bankruptcy. It is not a language of wisdom but rather ideological speech. This is not the place to quarrel about it, but when we see the fortunes used to cover bank frauds and bank games (very dangerous and ruinous speculations with the money of people who trusted them) and those used to attend to the needs of people we understand quite well who to blame about the crisis.

We must not have illusions about the place of law in this entire problem. The value of jurists in the general market has decreased severely since the times when they were ministers, counselors of kings and popes, and since other times where they were the real rulers, presidents, prime ministers, and the majority of the members of the parliaments. The Law itself lost its relative autonomy and is now more a machine of enforcing political decisions.

5.4 Lessons on Constitutional Theory: A Federal and Social Fraternal Europe

But there is still doctrine and jurists who are aware of their responsibilities: those who refuse to be mere bureaucrats of coercion. These jurists don't look the other way. They have built and are continuously building theoretical instruments to analyze realities and to translate Justice into real things. One of those tools is the concept of *material constitution*. Another is Karl Loewenstein's classification of constitutions according to their "normative force" in reality[5]: either a constitution is lived or it remains less more than just a sheet of paper (as Ferdinand de Lassalle once put it[6]). They can be normative (high level of practical application), nominal, or semantic (if they are not law in action).

And with the help of these concepts we may consider the present situation of crises running to a material unconstitutionality and a nominal or semantic application of treaties, namely the Lisbon treaty, which is the present European constitution.

The situation gives us a yearning for the future Europe: with an assumed Constitution without the fear of that word, federalist at all levels (taking seriously the principle of subsidiarity), and not only defending but also deepening the Social State. That would be the satisfactory equivalence among the material constitution, formal constitution, and real constitution: the spirit, the body, and the soul of European Constitution. And then Europe will be a republican Republic of republics (even if there are some monarchies in it). And its law a Law of brotherhood, not the severe and predatory and greedy *ius utendi, fruendi et abutendi.* Europe will be Free, Equal, and Fraternal. If not (as Aragon's barons once mythically said to the King of Leon and Castile when he invited them to join a major state) we may abridge into three words: *If not, not*. Or *Si no, no!* "Because each one of us has the same value of you, and altogether more than you—said Aragon's noblemen—we agree to join you", but with conditions … So, the myth says they entered as a part of Spain on the condition of respect for their laws and liberties.

What is sometimes going on in Barcelona makes many people suspect that that respect maybe was not real, or was not enough. And if not, *may be not* … The future shall give all the answers to our current anguished doubts. But the future is always in the People's hands. That's what popular sovereignty means. It is not an invention of insane utopianisms; it is a fact of History. And next History begins now.

---

5 Loewenstein (1969).

6 Lassalle (1862).

References

Lassalle, F. (1862). *Über Verfassungswesen* (in German), English translation, *On the essence of constitutions*, conference. http://www.gewaltenteilung.de/lassalle.htm. Retrieved April 16, 1862, from http://www.marxists.org/history/etol/newspape/fi/vol03/no01/lassalle.htm.

Loewenstein, K. (1969). *Verfassungslehre* (2nd ed.). Tübingen: J. C. B. Mohr (Paul Siebeck).

Mitterrand, D. (2007). *Le Livre de ma mémoire*. Paris: Gallimard.

Pereira-Menaut, A.-C. et al. (2000). *La Constitución europea: tratados constitutivos y jurisprudencia*. Santiago de Compostela: Universidade de Santiago de Compostela.

MIX
Papier aus verantwortungsvollen Quellen
Paper from responsible sources
FSC® C105338

If you have any concerns about our products,
you can contact us on
ProductSafety@springernature.com

In case Publisher is established outside the EU,
the EU authorized representative is:
Springer Nature Customer Service Center GmbH
Europaplatz 3, 69115 Heidelberg, Germany

Printed by Libri Plureos GmbH
in Hamburg, Germany